QUEER POETICS

QUEER
POETICS

Five
Modernist
Women
Writers

Mary E. Galvin

Contributions in Women's Studies, Number 161

GREENWOOD PRESS
Westport, Connecticut • London

Library of Congress Cataloging-in-Publication Data

Galvin, Mary E., 1961–
    Queer poetics : five modernist women writers / Mary E. Galvin.
      p. cm.—(Contributions in women's studies, ISSN 0147-104X ;
  no. 161)
    Includes bibliographical references and index.
    ISBN 0-313-29810-6 (alk. paper)
    1. Lesbians' writings, American—History and criticism.
  2. Dickinson, Emily, 1830–1886—Criticism and interpretation.
  3. Stein, Gertrude, 1874–1946—Criticism and interpretation.
  4. Lowell, Amy, 1874–1925—Criticism and interpretation.
  5. American poetry—Women authors—History and criticism.
  6. Homosexuality and literature—United States. 7. Barnes, Djuna—
  Criticism and interpretation. 8. Loy, Mina—Criticism and
  interpretation. 9. Modernism (Literature)—United States.
  10. Women and literature—United States. I. Title. II. Series.
  PS153.L46G35 1999
  810.9'9206643—dc21   97–21449

British Library Cataloguing in Publication Data is available.

A paperback edition of *Queer Poetics* is available from Praeger Publishers,
an imprint of Greenwood Publishing Group, Inc. (ISBN 0-275-96106-0).

Library of Congress Catalog Card Number: 97–21449
ISBN: 0-313-29810-6
ISSN: 0147-104X

First published in 1999

Greenwood Press, 88 Post Road West, Westport, CT 06881
An imprint of Greenwood Publishing Group, Inc.
www.greenwood.com

Printed in the United States of America

The paper used in this book complies with the
Permanent Paper Standard issued by the National
Information Standards Organization (Z39.48–1984).

10 9 8 7 6 5 4 3 2 1

CONSCIOUSNESS cannot spontaneously accept or reject new forms, as offered by creative genius; it is the new form, for however great a period of time it may remain a mere irritant—that molds consciousness to the necessary amplitude for holding it.

Mina Loy,
"Aphorisms On Futurism," 1914

The only thing that is different from one time to another is what is seen and what is seen depends upon how everybody is doing everything.

Gertrude Stein,
Composition as Explanation, 1926

9

Contents

Preface: Remembering

Make an effort to remember. Or, failing that, invent.
—Monique Wittig
Les Guerilleres, 1973

It was 1978 and I was 17. I had been craving poetry my whole life but had been fed only crumbs: a unit on Shakespeare, a day of funereal Dickinson, and periodically the Whitman who took a noble stance against war. When I moved from Catholic school to public school nothing was poetically different in the classroom, though among new friends, there were poems unearthed from the public library, and the expanding bookshelves of college-aged siblings. I was finally starting to find poems to chew on, poems that gnawed at me as being possible and real, poems that were not safe poems.

My head filled with *Howl*, and with the mostly white men a crazed generation before mine who forced their way into print and once there could curse and scream all they wanted. "Liberation of the word," Ginsberg called it. Next I encountered Nikki Giovanni, Gwendolyn Brooks, and Maya Angelou speaking of desire and hurt, of power and anger, writing themselves into strength and soul. White gay men, black straight women gave me the knowledge that poems that could sustain me were already written, were being written now. There was more than Carl Sandburg with his love of slaughter and industry to carry on from Whitman. There was a new Whitman emerging, and he had appeared to Ginsberg not long before in "A Supermarket in California."

My first encounter with homophobia in an institutional setting happened that year. Creative writing for seniors, and we could write an explication of any poem we chose. But not Ginsberg. I asked, and was told, "Not Ginsberg, because of his overt homosexuality." The teacher didn't know I was deeply involved in my first lesbian relationship with her other star pupil. She didn't know she had just slapped me with her "overt homophobia." I recovered and with rage I pored through Ginsberg's books until I found one—a poem for Vachel Lindsay—which was not "overt." My explication was written and turned in and graded favorably and not a further word on the topic was said.

In college, poetry seemed broader and more possible. I was finding friends who called themselves lesbian and who read poets not mentioned in class: Adrienne Rich, Pat Parker, Audre Lorde, Judy Grahn. They were an underground current, and yet they weren't secret. Their words and images were broadcast on posters in almost every dyke's home, on albums with the word *lesbian* printed boldly on the covers. It wasn't until the end of my second year that I encountered Rich in a classroom text, not the Rich I knew existed then, but the sixties protest poet who was diving into the wreck of what was once considered a viable culture with room for all. We could read Eldridge Cleaver's opinions on queers but never be told that Rich had become one.

Zoom into the future and I'm studying poets, theorists of criticism, and theorists of feminism. My chosen poets are a list of mostly forgotten women. I'm looking for my predecessors, for women writers who were doing something different for their day. Drawn initially by their poetics, I begin to learn also about their lives. By chance, I discover that nine out of ten of my choices were lesbian or bisexual, and although the tenth, Mina Loy, was ostensibly straight, most of her associates were one way or another queer, including her second husband. By chance? There's something more to this choosing than accident. There's a pattern, an aesthetic that's beginning to emerge.

That pattern, that aesthetic comes out of necessity. In a culture structured significantly by heterosexism, the mind that can imagine other sexualities and gender identities must also imagine other ways of speaking, new forms to articulate our visions of difference. In a cultural setting that deems us unthinkable, we've had to imagine our own existence.

Acknowledgments

I want to thank everyone who generously shared their time and insight with me as I worked, often at times more convenient for me than for them: Judith Johnson, Ron Bosco, Joan Schulz for their steady guidance, Jill Hanifan for proofreading and discussion and encouragement when I needed it most. I've received much support from many friends, in this, and everything, but I especially want to thank Penny Dugan, Paula Surdi, Diane Lunde, Nancy Klepsch, Lori Anderson, and again, Jill. But most of all, I want to thank Susan Shafarzek, for all of the above, and much much more.

Introduction: Lesbian Theory in Poetry

> The discourses which particularly oppress all of us, lesbians, women, and homosexual men, are those which take for granted that what founds society, any society, is heterosexuality....I would like to insist on the material oppression of individuals by discourses
>
> —Monique Wittig
> *The Straight Mind, 1992*

Lesbians in literature, as in life, are rarely seen. This is not to say that we don't exist, but only that in the traditional, phallocentric economy of representation, lesbian existence tends to be erased, overwritten by heterosexist assumptions.

This tendency is particularly operative in literature studies, where, even as the traditional boundaries of canon formation are being expanded to include writings by women, it is still deemed irrelevant, if not out-and-out taboo, to consider sexual orientation as a factor of interpretation. Lesbians, gay men, and bisexual people have consistently been canonized by the literary establishment—as long as their sexuality was not readily evident in their work, as long as the literary establishment could deny the relevance of their nonheterosexual identity. In fact, many scholars have gone out of their way to deny gay and lesbian existence in literature altogether. For example, they have searched for evidence of the "definitively" female identity of Shakespeare's beloved in the sonnets, or amassed ill-founded speculations on the "definitively" male identity of Emily Dickinson's "Master."

In spite of this silence on the part of the literary establishment, we've still been able to find some lesbians in literature: Sappho, Gertrude Stein, H.D. (a bisexual), Emily Dickinson (perhaps), Virginia Woolf (sometimes), May Sarton (eventually), Radclyffe Hall, Natalie Barney, Renee Vivien. In 1979, 1980, our canon was slim and often it seemed we were reaching. We knew there were predecessors if only through inference, by our own existence as lesbians. If only they would come out to us, if only we could discover them now.

Reconstructing an intellectual, cultural history that has been ignored, vilified, and erased is a necessary aspect of our empowerment. We've always known that many poets and writers throughout literary history have been "homosexual." However, in the mainstream classroom, in the mainstream texts, when this is mentioned (if it is mentioned at all), it is usually with a dismissive embarrassment, as if to say, "But that does not detract from the value of their contribution."

In effect, this "tolerant" approach acknowledges a writer's difference, only to dismiss its relevance. The conveyors of the traditional canon want to act as if this "difference" makes no difference at all in the way we read. The implication is that unless the writer's homosexuality is the "overt" subject of the poem, her queerness does not contribute to the artistic vision in any significant way. Once again, it can be safely ignored.

However, a "who's who" approach—a sort of historical "outing"—carries its own limitations. Every poem enacts a theory of language and consciousness. It creates or confirms a poetics through its form. Using a theory of reading based on a theory of the poet's identity, it is too easy to disregard the significance of the poetic form.

It's not enough to read for symbols, coded messages, oblique references to being queer. What if the poet is known to have been gay but never mentions this fact in the work, even in coded form? What if poets change sexuality in midcareer? Were they writing as queers before they were loving that way? Did Allen Ginsberg stop writing from his "overt homosexuality" when his poem to Vachel Lindsay was sadly tender, full of stars rather than his usually more explicit sexual terms? Could I read Adrienne Rich's earlier work as the work of a lesbian even if she were living as a heterosexual when it was written? A more subtle rubric is required.

If heterosexism were not the hidden ruling category in our culture, we would have, among other things, a language that could describe more than two gender categories. If heterosexuality had no need to assert itself as the privileged term in the binary opposition heterosexual/homosexual, the words "homosexual" or "lesbian" would not be made to carry the implications of sexual deviance, social taboo. Under the heterosexist system, the factors of genital structure and sexual practice serve as the primary ground of categorical distinctions among people: woman/man, straight/gay. This preoccupation with sex, and its allegedly "natural" and "universal" precondition, the maintenance of clearly defined gender distinctions "works specifically, as 'black' does, through an operation of reduction, by taking the part for the whole, a part (color, sex) through which the whole human being has to pass as through a screen" (Wittig 1992:44).

As a culture, the heterosexual order is obsessed with this metonymic (dis)placement of beings; the practice of categorizing is a fetishizing practice. The heterosexist society imbues its fetish (gender, sex) with inordinate power, the power of the universal, the ahistorical, the transcultural, the power of original immutable truth. The fetish, which by definition is a small portion of the whole, becomes the founding principle of a worldview, and it brings to bear all the righteousness and might of a political regime to enforce this view "universally." In doing so, the fetishizing practices of heterosexist thinking condemn the possibility of diversity, variety, or multiplicity as "deviance": inversion, perversion, corruption, or illness is made to reside within the political transgressor's inner being, a constitutional flaw, rather than a conscious choice to resist the social order of heterosexist thinking. To live outside the boundaries of binary oppositions a different kind of thinking is necessary, and new theorists with it.

From the beginning of our contemporary movements for liberation and visibility, poets have been among our major cultural workers. They have spoken for us and to us, and they have helped us all remember and claim our names. "So it is better to speak/remembering/we were never meant to survive," wrote Audre Lorde.[1] Contemporary lesbian poets have had a distinct advantage over most of their predecessors. Not only could they be overt in their poetry, but they could also be theorists of homosexuality.

In her "Transcendental Etude" Adrienne Rich spoke of "a whole new poetry beginning here." Since the mid-1970s, a revolution of poetics and consciousness and knowledge has been happening within the lesbian community, and it is continuing at full strength today.[2] It is a poetics of disruption, of crossing boundaries, of dismantling categorical distinctions. In speaking of and from our multiple differences—the differences we experience among ourselves within our communities as well as the differences we assert from the heterosexual order—it is a poetics that embraces and fosters a transformative vision of complexity in the world. Our poets are our theorists— theorists of language and form ("the difference between poetry and rhetoric," as Audre Lorde called it), theorists of the interrelationship of language, consciousness, sexuality, and social control, theorists of the deconstruction of categorical thinking, theorists of gender and identity and the unconscious.

Rich's essay, "Compulsory Heterosexuality and the Continuum of Lesbian Existence" first published in 1978, set off a theoretical debate that has not yet abated. I first encountered this essay, along with Lorde's essay, "Uses of the Erotic: The Erotic as Power" in 1982. Taken together, the two essays shook up our inherited sense of categorical definitions. They began to blur boundaries of sexuality and gender that mainstream straight culture insists are immutable, even as we know differently from our own lives.[3]

Rich's theory opened up the possibility of reading beyond the oppressors' "clinical definitions" of lesbianism "to include a range—through each woman's life and throughout history—of woman-identified experience, not simply the fact that a woman has had or consciously desired genital experience with another woman" (51). Lorde's theory enabled us to expand our understanding of our erotic energies beyond the heterosexual definitions, to understand that the focus of our oppression as women generally and as lesbians in particular has been deliberately geared toward dismantling the erotic source of our power, narrowing its scope and then turning it against us.

To undermine the heterosexist order at its base, it is necessary to de-fetishize sex, to divest it of its metonymic powers, and its service in the construction of reductive, categorically manipulated identities, to subvert its strength as a means of social and political control. When Adrienne Rich argues in "Compulsory Heterosexuality" that we need to shift our understanding of the term *lesbian* from its rigid, sex-obsessed clinical definition to include the various means women have discovered, throughout history and across cultures, to resist compliance to the heterosexual order, she is "universalizing" what has been previously seen as "deviant," and is "politicizing" what had previously been seen as "natural."

In doing so, Rich is pushing the concept of the deviant, the anomalous, the lesbian beyond the reductivism of categorical thinking toward a more expansive conceptual framework, that of the "continuum." This continuum is not of identity or "mere lifestyle," but of "existence," being: a shift from fixation with the part to consideration of the whole.

When Rich insists on the word *continuum*, when she adds the word *existence* after lesbian, she is asking all feminists, straight, gay, or other, to shun the politicized sexual fetish as our organizing principal, to forego the convenience of categorizing people metonymically, to shift the center of the debate. She asks us to shift our focus from the reductivism of the sex fetish to the role this fetish is forced to play in a culture structured by heterosexuality, to look at its function in a political framework.

Heterosexuality is compulsory for all. There are numerous institutional controls of the body and of the mind, ranging from economic oppression to rape, which uphold the heterosexualized social structure. These controls affect all "women" and any "deviant" men, regardless of their "sexual preferences."

With her phrase, "the continuum of lesbian existence," Rich is asking all feminist thinkers to shift our mode of analysis, of conceptualizing identity, away from narrow categorical distinctions to a more expansive notion of a continuum of existence, an existence created in our resistance to the institutional boundaries of heterosexuality.

The irony of this discursive situation is that the heterosexist system of binary oppositions views the endless variety of resistance to heterosexism monolithically. Here, the views of Monique Wittig have particular relevance. If one locates oneself as the center of discourse, as the universal, the norm, all the variations of nonheterosexist identity can be casually lumped together as the marginal, the other, the deviant, the queer. This attitude Wittig has called "the straight mind."

According to the straight mind's version of the unconscious, any rejection of the validity of its symbols and processes not only results in "abnormal" or "deviant" sexuality in the individual, but is tantamount to rejecting the "symbolic order" through which meaning, sexuality, and society itself is founded. And this, we are told, is "impossible":

In this thought, to reject the obligation of coitus and the institutions this obligation has produced as necessary for the constitution of a society, is simply an impossibility, since to do this would mean to reject the possibility of the constitution of the other and to reject the "symbolic order," to make the constitution of meaning impossible, without which no one can maintain an internal coherence. Thus lesbianism, homosexuality, and the societies that we form cannot be thought of or spoken of, even though they have always existed. Thus, the straight mind continues to affirm that incest, and not homosexuality, represents its major interdiction. Thus, when thought by the straight mind, homosexuality is nothing but heterosexuality. (Wittig 1992:28)

When a violent heterosexist wants to gay bash, it makes little difference whether the victim defines herself as a lesbian or a bisexual, or simply has been seen out with people who do. But those who reside in the "margins" perceive differences along the lines of a seemingly endless diversity, multiplicity, differences among, not a reductivist difference from. It is this perception of multiple otherness which the straight mind with its reductivist dual-gender system cannot address. The dichotomizing, categorical mode of establishing identity metonymically is inadequate to expressing the knowledge of the "queer mind."

The fact is that multifarious difference does and always has existed; this difference has been overlooked, distorted, or out-and-out denied. Since the system of binary oppositions (and its concomitant institutions of social/sexual control) cannot accommodate more than one pair of gender differences, the straight mind would choose to deny even the possibility of multiplicity. Failing that, the straight mind would convert us into deviant heterosexuals, sorry parodies of the "natural order." What the straight mind continually fails to see is that lesbian and gay identity steps well beyond the realm of dichotomous distinctions and is often quite self-aware in doing so. We do not want to re-create identity for ourselves based on the model of heterosexuality. On the contrary: our existence depends on a rejection of the heterosexual terms of identity, for it is those terms that deem us "unthinkable" and "impossible."

In my own journey of re-envisioning and renaming lesbian identity and consciousness, I have often been drawn back to the period of the modernists. While I was learning the "straight," mostly male, modernist tradition in college and also learning, somewhat haphazardly, of the women writing then, I was struck by how many were lesbian, bisexual, or nonheterocentric in their lives: Gertrude Stein, H.D., Bryher, Edna St. Vincent Millay, Amy Lowell, Natalie Barney, Renee Vivien, Laura Riding, Mina Loy, Djuna Barnes. Many of them knew and interacted with each other. I began to imagine the mutual influences they must have had, even when antagonistic at times.

In the early decades of the twentieth century, artists and writers gathered in cities such as Paris, Florence, Berlin, London, and New York. Concurrently, lesbians and gay men began to gather in metropolitan communities. Often the two groups were not separate but inextricably related, at times indistinguishable.

As Lillian Faderman, Michel Foucault, and others have indicated, we can trace the origins of our contemporary "gay consciousness" to this period.[4] For a variety of social, cultural, and economic reasons, gay people, poets, artists, musicians, bohemians, social deviants, and queers of all sorts began to leave their home towns and meet each other and live and work together in the major cities of the United States and Europe. From the beginning, the development of modernist consciousness and gay consciousness has been intertwined. It's time to take the influence of sexual politics into account in the ways we reconstruct modernism in our literary histories.

In thinking of our queer modernist predecessors, I like to keep in mind Adrienne Rich's continuum and her assertion that "a feminism of action, often though not always without a theory, has constantly re-emerged in every culture and in every period.... We can begin to observe behavior which often constitutes, given the limits of the counterforce exerted in a given time and place, radical rebellion" (57).

Inevitably, this rebellion can take a variety of forms. We need theories that are expansive enough to include all of them, so that the erasures and dismissals, the deliberate ignorance and misreading of our history as gay, lesbian, or queer people does not continue to happen. Just as a variety of sexualities are possible in the realm of the nonheterosexual, so our writers have developed a variety of poetics to articulate our hard-won "differences."

The means of resistance to the straight mind's constructs are various, and, most often, discovered and carried out on an individual basis. In her essay, "On the Social Contract," Monique Wittig writes, "I have always thought that women are a class structured very much as was the class of serfs. I see now that they can tear themselves away from the heterosexual order only by running away one by one" (1992:34). Obviously, under a heterosexist regime, there is no clear path *away* from heterosexuality, but it is made relatively easy to find your way to it. Our conception of what it means to be lesbian, to be gay, to be nonheterosexual must be able to encompass the variety of forms these struggles against the heterosexist order have taken, are taking, and will take. Gertrude Stein, for example, did not write or live in the same way as Djuna Barnes, and I could not, and would not want, to read them in the same way. Yet, I find in each of them a poetics that disrupts the pretended stability and "naturalness" of the heterosexist worldview.

Given the ways that heterosexist thinking clings to dualism, it becomes clear why queer existence must struggle so hard against cultural invisibility and erasure. The heterosexist order has dismissed lesbian existence as trivial, or has persecuted it as dangerously perverse. To acknowledge and embrace nonheterocentric existence in its full significance creates much complexity in the world; it upsets the social order.

By definition, queer subjects (and I include all nonheterocentrically defined identities here) take a revolutionary stance against the patriarchal order by refusing to be heterosexually identified, by rejecting its dualisms as the basis of truth, and by refusing to create their lives in the traditionally-cast mold of gender distinctions. In reconstructing a literary history, theorizing a queer cultural aesthetic, I am reading for the many ways there are to undermine a hierarchy, to subvert a falsely coherent heterocentric regime.

Once one begins to live and think outside the categorical boundaries of binary oppositions, anything is possible. In order to exist and to write that existence, lesbians and other nonheterocentrically defined people have had to make ourselves thinkable in order to be possible.

The writers at the center of this study are all nonheterocentric in their personal identities. They are also all innovators of modernist poetics. My basic assumption in this work is that the mind which can imagine other sexual orientations and gender identities can and must also imagine new ways of writing.

I begin with a consideration of Emily Dickinson as a sexually deviant precursor to the modernists. Through close reading of a handful of her poems, I hope to establish not so much the lesbian identity of Dickinson, but the fact that her poetic innovations were necessitated by a desire to establish a nonheterosexual identity for herself. Dickinson inhabited the hymn meter—the most solid and single-minded form available to her—and disrupted syntax, formal meter, and rhyme. In so doing, she transformed the duplicity of language from a medium of coding and disguise into a technique for questioning and undermining the certainty of all boundaries, all categorical distinctions. These techniques also provided the poetic groundwork for the modernists whose poetics comprise the rest of my study.

The erasure of Amy Lowell from her rightful place in the literary canon is due, I believe, to a homophobic reaction to her overt lesbianism. Lowell's development of experimental techniques once made her famous as a major practitioner and promoter of modernist poetics in the United States. Nevertheless, Lowell's poetry, like Dickinson's can be, and has been, misconstrued at various junctures, as trivial and focussed primarily on nature in the most banal sense. In Chapter 2, I discuss Lowell's poetics of imagism as a technique that enabled her not only to write extremely erotic lesbian poetry, but also to explore the power of the erotic in an expansive sense. The invisibility of lesbian eroticism to the heterosexist eye has allowed mainstream critics to ignore this central aspect of Lowell's poetics. In addition to her focussed use of image, Lowell worked in other forms. As with Dickinson, Lowell subversively inhabited conventional form, in this case the long narrative poem of the New England story-telling tradition. Under Lowell's pen, the form is made to accommodate techniques of imagism, thereby enabling her to explore issues of sexual politics as they related to the emergent modernist consciousness of her day. Lowell also created a form called "Polyphonic Prose," a technique that has certain connections with the syntactic and linguistic experiments of both Dickinson and Stein. While the actual strategy of disruption is different from Dickinson's—"Polyphonic Prose" works through an accumulation of language rather than a sparseness—it also works toward undermining categorical distinctions, dissolving the distinction between poetic and prosaic discourses. Lowell's "Polyphonic Prose" was conceived as performance poetry and is specifically geared toward eliciting a sensual and emotional response from the reader/audience. In doing so, Lowell brings lesbian eroticism and a crossing of genre boundaries together with a disruption of traditional hierarchical distinctions between poet and audience.

While the lesbian identity of Gertrude Stein is well established, most critics have not considered this fact as relevant to her writing. In Chapter 3, I explore the ways Stein breaks down the distinction between author and reader in the search for "meaning." Stein, like Lowell, was also concerned with undermining the hierarchical relationship established conventionally through the creation of literature. Like Dickinson, Stein disrupted categorical definitions of "meaning" by playing with the duplicity of language (its potential for ambiguity, equivocation, unstable meanings). In doing so, both poets created not an absence of meaning but a multiplicity. Stein's concept of a "continuous present," achieved through disrupting conventional syntax and creating new linguistic forms by which consciousness could express itself, also creates an alternative means of conceptualizing personal identity. In Stein, this reconceptualization coincided with the need to speak of/from her lesbian consciousness. Through her techniques of disruption, Stein created a poetics that portrays an ever-changing self, never definable to others, never transparent or stable to one's self. It is a self that exists beyond the boundaries of categorical distinctions.

In Chapter 4, I consider the poetics of Mina Loy, who did not identify herself as lesbian. Her main relevance to this study is her deconstruction of the paradigm that she found to be one of the most persistent forms of oppression, even within the so-called sexual revolution of her day. She not only associated with lesbians and other queer modernists, but in her work she enacted a strong questioning of the heterosexist paradigm. Throughout her career, Loy consistently explored issues of sexuality and gender identity. Her work comprises a powerful critique of traditional love and romance as a textual creation of phallocentric discourses. She accomplished this by inhabiting the tradition of the "love poem" disruptively, much in the way Dickinson inhabited the hymn form. In both her life and her work, Loy displayed several other continuities with Dickinson's strategies for nullifying the confines of heterocentric thinking, though in a modernist setting. A major proponent of modernist poetic techniques, Loy was the innovator of the extremely narrow free verse line and the use of empty space within a line. In utilizing these techniques, Loy opened up the poetic line to new possibilities of significance, through a combination of precise word choice and ambiguously disrupted syntax, thus enabling her to explore new forms of consciousness, sexual identity, and ways of conceptualizing the "self."

Although in her later years Djuna Barnes denied her lesbianism ("I'm not a lesbian. I just loved Thelma"),[5] both the facts of her life and the evidence of her writings belie this statement. Barnes' awareness of heterosexist oppression, combined with the complexity of her vision, led her to personally resist easy categorization. She is best known for *Nightwood*, a "novel" in which she breaks down traditional distinctions between genres, in order to explore the dreamlike, liminal space of the "third sex." This same theme runs consistently through the bulk of her work, although most critics choose to ignore its import. In Chapter 5, I focus primarily on Barnes' earliest work, *The Book of Repulsive Women*, which centers on lesbian characters and the effects heterosexist oppression has in their lives. In *The Book of Repulsive Women*, Barnes, perhaps more than any other poet I discuss, is strikingly similar to Dickinson in her ability to transform the ambiguity of language from a medium of coding and disguise into a technique for disrupting the certainty of categorical boundaries. In these poems, as well as all her subsequent works, Barnes also developed a technique of reappropriating "archaic" language styles and forms by which she could write lesbianism into literary existence. Like Dickinson, in *The Book of Repulsive Women*, Barnes utilized a strategy of disruptively inhabiting formal meter and rhyme to undermine formal boundaries and expectations, thereby clearing a space for a multiplicitous, nonheterocentric thinking.

While it has always been fairly well known that H.D. was bisexual, critics and biographers have tended to emphasize the significance of her heterosexual relationships to her poetic development. By focusing on the heterosexual aspects of her life and work, the questioning of her identity as a woman under that paradigm overshadows any questioning of her identity as a lesbian under a heterosexist regime. In Chapter 6, I offer a reassessment of H.D.'s career, which I believe coincides more closely with the terms by which she herself defined her life and work. More recent critics, such as Robert Duncan and Eileen Gregory, have suggested that the disreputable figure of "the Poetess" has overshadowed H.D.'s reputation even among her critical advocates. However, if we revise our image of the Poetess from the meek, overly sensitive "lady poet" to an image of the self-empowering shaman-poet—seeking her history and attempting to convey her apprehension of nonheterocentric consciousness—H.D.'s use of personae, indirection, ambiguity, and paradox can be seen as deliberately chosen techniques for conveying her insights with as much clarity as possible. Motivated by the need to open up social/intellectual/psychic space for queer existence, H.D. sought, in the new freedom of modernism, to piece together the significance of her personal experiences through the techniques of imagism, within the palimpsest of myth.

Throughout this book, I have relied interpretively on the work of contemporary queer poet/theorists, in the hope of establishing continuity among the poetic themes and techniques intiated by queer modernists and those theories articulated and utilized by more recent queer poets. My own method of reading, in any literary period, has been strongly influenced by my training in post-structuralist approaches, especially deconstruction, as well as the theoretical insights articulated past fifteen years or so under the rubric "Queer Theory." However, these influences comprise more of the backbone of my approach than the flesh, and I very rarely make direct reference to post-structuralism or queer theory within my text. My choice to privilege poets over more academically-oriented critical theorists is meant, not to devalue the significance of critical theory, but to assert positively the significance of certain poets' contributions to the development of a queer critical consciousness.

In addition, in researching other critics' involvement with the writers in my study, I have often found that queer poets have provided a starting point more strongly relevant to my project than other critics' approaches to these writers. To date, much of the criticism written by contemporary queer theorists and poststructuralists has been centered mostly on the interpretation of popular culture, fiction, and autobiography. The application of these approaches to reading poetry, especially poetry written in the modernist period, has just begun.

With this in mind, I would like to acknowledge the limits of the scope of this book. For each poet I chose to focus a chapter on, I have been painfully aware of the dozens of other potential candidates for study. From the beginning of the twentieth century until the present, many poets have exceeded the boundaries of heterocentric identity and epistemology in their poetics, not only these few who associated themselves with the "high modernists." I have not delved into the queer poetics in the works of American women of color, nonheterocentric males of any race, certain political and social protest poets of this century, or our current queer poets of the avante-garde. I am hoping this book will contribute positively to this growing field, and will encourage readers and critics into further explorations of the intersections between "gay consciousness" and experimental poetic techniques throughout our literary history.

NOTES

1.   Lorde, "A Litany for Survival," in *The Black Unicorn* (New York: W. W. Norton, 1978), 32.

2.   Rich, *The Dream of a Common Language: Poems 1974–1977* (New York: W. W. Norton, 1978), 76.

3.   These essays are now available in the following collections: Rich, *Blood, Bread and Poetry: Selected Prose, 1979-1985* (New York: W. W. Norton, 1986); Lorde, *Sister Outsider* (Trumansburg, N. Y.: Crossing Press, 1984).

4.   Faderman, *Odd Girls and Twilight Lovers* (New York: Penguin, 1991); Foucault, *The History of Sexuality, Volume 1: An Introduction* (New York: Vintage Books, 1990).

5.   Andrew Field, *Djuna: The Life and Times of Djuna Barnes* (New York: Putnam, 1983), 37.

CHAPTER 1

Poltergeist of Form: Emily Dickinson and the Reappropriation of Language and Identity

Most people are familiar with the traditional interpretation of the life of Emily Dickinson (1830-1886). Meek, soft-spoken, and deferential, painfully shy—the story goes—this "half-cracked poetess" withdrew from the world at large into the safety of her father's genteel household. Eccentric in appearance and mannerism, she wore mostly white, especially in later years, and spent her days in reclusive spinsterhood, remaining in a perpetual childhood. Her only responsibilities were to bake the daily bread for the family and to care for her invalid mother. The rest of her days were spent wandering through the garden and retiring to her room to compose pretty little nature poems that she rarely sent out, apparently because she knew her erratic sense of meter was not of professional caliber.[1]

Evidently, she was also excessively sensitive, to the point of a neurotic morbidity, since many of her poems are marked by a preoccupation with death, pain, and funerals. She must have suffered some great tragic loss early on in her adulthood, which informed the painful aspects of her vision. This secret tragedy must have been romantic in nature, since no other adventure than heterosexual romance could possibly have crossed her path.

Pouring her passionate powers into her poetry, the myth tells us, Dickinson created a few gems (surprisingly, given the limits of her education and life experiences), but produced many half-finished oddities, or overwritten, emotionally excessive pieces, which in both cases she was wise not to publish. In fact, after her death, most of these were considered not worthy of print, and of the few that were deemed worthwhile, many were thought to require the educated skills of an editor. Apparently, she had an awful sense of syntax and punctuation, and often lost control of both her subject and her meter altogether.

Thus reads the heterosexist myth of Emily Dickinson, viewed as the dutiful (heterosexual) daughter of the fathers.[2] But if we shift our understanding of Dickinson by placing her on the continuum of lesbian existence, we can begin to appreciate her resourcefulness in resisting the compulsory subservence of women under heterosexism and fathom the source of her prolific and peculiar creativity. Her life is no longer pathetic and odd, but imbued with the radical strength and vision of an autonomous female, living and creating to the best of her ability within the confines of nineteenth-century ideology. Once we begin to move away from heterosexist assumptions, our interpretations of her poetry inevitably shift as well. When we look at her from the vantage point of sexual politics, Dickinson can be seen no longer as a troubled, but dutiful daughter of the patriarchy, but as a lesbian who both needed and wanted to disrupt the linguistic and epistemological structures of phallocentrism in order to speak her (queer) mind.

Dickinson was enamored with the expansive powers of the mind. No poem states this belief as clearly as poem 632, "The Brain— is wider than the Sky—." Like her contemporary, Whitman, she insists that the grandeur and knowledge traditionally reserved for God exists within the human mind. Both poets held beliefs that were considered heretical by contemporary religious standards, and both poets experienced the need to disrupt traditional poetics, particularly in regard to meter, in order to express this vision. I believe it is no accident that the two poets to which we, as late twentieth-century scholars, trace the origins of modernist poetics in America chose to live in resistence to the material and representational economies of traditional heterosexuality.

In order to see their way clear of the strictures of nineteenth-century poetics, they had to have already occupied a position of defiance, in their sense of self and their understanding of how identity is constructed, as well as in their sense of reality and their understanding of the construction of the world.

The similarities to be drawn between these two sexual rebels are limited by the differences imposed on them by the circumstance of gender. Whitman, as a strapping young American male, experiences in himself and in his world a plenitude, which is reflected in his prosody. Long, end-stopped lines, full of sensual images of life and abundance came from a luxury of gender privilege. As a male, Whitman was free to roam the country at large, an endeavor that would likely have left Dickinson, as a female, raped and starved, subsequently to be either enslaved or left for dead. Given that Dickinson's survival, in a most literal sense, was dependent on at least a modicum of acquiescence to her family's and her society's expectations, she made herself over in the only unconstrained image available to her, the quiet spinster, just that little bit odd so that no one would challenge her single (and singular) state.

Whitman could afford an openly defiant stance toward the authority of tradition and was able to assume his own exuberant authority in its stead. As a result, nature, sex, bodies, the self, and its senses fill his lines so that they overflow the margins of the page and have to be continued below. This option was not available to Dickinson, who lurked behind the confines of tradition, but escaped its punitive strictures through the expansive powers of the mind.

> They shut me up in Prose—
> As when a little Girl
> They put me in the Closet—
> Because they liked me "still"—
>
> Still! Could themself have peeped—
> And seen my Brain—go round—
> They might as wise have lodged a Bird
> For Treason—in the Pound—
>
> Himself has but to will
> And easy as a Star
> Abolish his Captivity—
> And laugh—No more have I—
> (J, 613)[3]

In this poem, Dickinson is clearly drawing an analogy between the socialization process of women and the strictures of "proper" language use, and is defiant toward both. Obviously, by being a poet, Dickinson has resisted her confinement to "prose," a form considered more suitable to the limitations of the female mind than the rigorous demands of poetry. Thus, in overstepping the bounds of genre, Dickinson is simultaneously overstepping the boundaries of gender. Although the stanza is brief, Dickinson manages to convey the brutality implicit in the socialization of women to ensure their poetic silence. For not keeping one's mouth shut, for refusing to be seen but not heard, which in itself is a punishing, oppressive attitude, the little girl is subjected to forced confinement. Physical violence is a requisite corollary to the violence of indoctrination into the prosaic world of "sense."

Yet she laughs, or sneers, in the second stanza, with the confidence of one who knows otherwise, one who sees the futility of this attempt at confinement. Her brain is in motion and cannot be stilled any more than a bird can be held in by fences. The charge of "Treason" indicates her awareness of the political implications of her resistance to this confinement. At the same time, she is asserting the absurdity of such a charge to one who is beyond political or social allegiances. Like a bird, Dickinson is "disloyal to civilization."

The oppression is only effective in keeping her brain still if she believes it, and accepts her captor's thinking. By willing against it from within her mind, she can fly away, and in a doubly treasonous act, she can defy even the charges of treason by which she is initially confined. At the end, her laugh of defiance is coupled with the assertion of her ability to escape as the bird does, through mental determination or will. The dash with which she "ends" the poem is a poetic enactment of her resistance to confinement, by resisting closure. Many of Dickinson's poems "end" with a dash, leaving the conclusion open-ended, ongoing, and capable of sustaining multiple interpretations. In this poem, the dash indicates the continuation of the process of resistance, the fact that the struggle against socialization is ongoing, its outcome indeterminable.

At the same time, the dash heightens the ambiguity of meaning in the final phrase, "No more have I—." Does she mean she has no more difficulty than a bird or a star does in evading captivity, that she can do so with ease? Or does she mean that she has no more will, that the punitive system of socialization has robbed her of will altogether? As a child she had the strength to resist, but now she has it "No more"? Given that she wrote this poem in her adulthood, I would lean toward the former interpretation, but I also see it as implying the limited nature of her resources for resistance. She has little physical strength or money, and no political power to aid in her resistance; she must carry on the struggle with no other resources than her will.

"Tell all the Truth but tell it slant—/Success in Circuit lies," Dickinson wrote, and it is this strategy of coded speech that won her what autonomy she could wrest from her circumstances. One of her most consistently utilized strategies of successful circuitry lies in her use of the hymn, or "common" meter, in conjunction with the preponderance of religious language and symbolism. As the daughter of a highly religious man, not only would she be well versed in the forms of piety, but the subversion of these forms would constitute the most immediate strategy of rebellion. This allowed Dickinson to express her rebellion on a highly personal level as well as on an expansively political level. In regard to religion, the forces of personal experience and of institutional control coincide in the life of Emily Dickinson.

> I'm ceded—I've stopped being Theirs—
> The name They dropped upon my face
> With water, in the country church
> Is finished using, now,
> And They can put it with my Dolls,
> My childhood, and the string of spools,
> I've finished threading—too—
>
> Baptized, before, without the choice,
> But this time, consciously, of Grace—
> Unto supremest name—
> Called to my Full—The Crescent dropped—
> Existence's whole Arc, filled up,
> With one small Diadem.
>
> My second Rank—too small the first—
> Crowned—Crowing—on my Father's breast—
> A half unconscious Queen—
> But this time—Adequate—Erect,
> With Will to choose, or to reject,
> And I choose, just a Crown—
>   (J, 508)

In "I'm ceded—I've stopped being Theirs—" Dickinson makes an explicit rejection of one of the initiation rituals of patriarchal religion, that is, baptism. The power of this institution's control over language and identity is acknowledged in her specific rejection of "The name They dropped upon my face." In a typical Dickinsonian move, however, she builds a syntactical ambiguity into the stanza with the fourth line: "Is finished using, now." Are we to read it as *she* is finished using the name now? Or that *it* (the name) is finished using her now? In either case, use of the name is done with now, but the ambiguity of agent/object in the line creates a complexity rich in implications, by the simple omission of a pronoun. For Dickinson, such clear-cut binary distinctions need to be problematized. Tellingly, her rejection of the religious rite and its power to name is juxtaposed in this stanza with her rejection of the female socialization process, indicated by the dolls of childhood and the women's work of threading spools. The three systems of social control are mutually supportive, and Dickinson is well aware of the interconnections among the power of naming, the dogma of traditional Christianity, and the social construction of "femininity."

It is interesting to note the role that "They" play in this as well as in other poems. Although Dickinson is using a seemingly ambiguous pronoun by not providing us with a proper referent, it soon becomes very clear that "They" are her own family members. "They" are the ones who name her and have control over the things of her childhood. The most significant part of her relationship to "Them" in terms of sexual politics, however, is that "They" have tried to own her, and it is this possessive power that is the first ground of her rejection: "I've stopped being Theirs—." This resistance implies, again by the use of a political term (ceded), the definitively political nature of this rejection. Even as we can deduce that in this poem "They" represent the people who would have the most immediate control over her life, her family members, the ambiguity of the pronoun serves a further purpose. In colloquial terms, "They" is often used to represent the power structures of society itself. "They" are the legislators of life, the unseen yet fully felt powers that institute an oppressive ideology. It is a given that Dickinson would have experienced "Their" interdiction even if she had left her close family circle, whether "They" took the form of a husband, lover, minister, politician, or editor. In short, "They," when taken as the agents of sexual and linguistic oppression, are everywhere in the world at large, and the only space where "They" can be denied the right of occupation is within Dickinson's own mind.

Throughout the second and third stanzas here, the issue of choice becomes central to the poem. Denied choice in the original baptism, she is now asserting her own power and right to choose. As in 613, "They shut me up in Prose—," it is "With Will to choose, or to reject," that she will overcome the control "They" have imposed on her being. Now conscious of her ability to choose, Dickinson will choose the "supremest name," that of a poet, enabled to name herself. In this choice she is "Called to my Full—" and although the phrasing here is incomplete (full what? potential? being? name?), it is clear that her choice gives her a sense of plenitude. Yet this plenitude is marked by irony. For it is the crescent moon, the Arc of Existence, the incomplete whole that can be "filled up." The sense of plenitude that Dickinson conveys here is not based on completion and closure, but is born out of incompletion, potentiality, a sense of plenitude as an ongoing process, as amplitude.

Defiantly crowned and crowing from her "Father's breast—," literally, the "heart" of patriarchy and its religious dictates, she will (consciously) choose to be "A half unconscious Queen—." The oxymoron implied here indicates to some degree the complexity of Dickinson's vision. For consciousness—awareness of her power to choose—involves also an awareness of the unconscious, and its power to inform both life choices and the powers of poetic vision. If a poet refuses to acknowledge the power of the unconscious in her life, she will cut herself off from one of the most important sources of poetic knowledge. It is with this both/and vision, of living in the space between and beyond the dichotomous distinction conscious/unconscious without deeming these two states to be mutually exclusive, that she has full power. In an appropriation of sexual imagery of male power, she names herself as "Adequate—Erect," even as she chooses the "Crown" of a "Queen," a decidedly female image. By blending the genders implied by these words of power, Dickinson is subverting the distinctions between genders, a move that is relevant to her choice to be a woman poet. In choosing such a crown, she is choosing her own laurels, the crown of a poet, once again empowered only by her "Will to choose, or to reject." In choosing to be such a Queen, she will maintain power over herself with a self-given name and role, not one bestowed on her by others.

In a final ironic twist to this poem, Dickinson again selects a strange locution to represent her choice. The last line ends with a dash, implying an indeterminate outcome. But the phrase preceding this "final" dash "just a Crown—" creates an indeterminacy of meaning. Does "just" mean "such," as in "just the crown such as I've been discussing?" Or does she mean "only," as in "I could have chosen a role even more powerful than that of poet/Queen, but in all my modesty, I will limit myself to choosing 'just a Crown?'" True to her strategy of slanting the truth even as she tells it, Dickinson's line can sustain either interpretation.

Dickinson's propensity for the hymn, or common meter, and its variants (e.g., short measure, long hymnal measure, etc.) has in itself led to varying interpretations of her poetic skill. Some of these interpretations are purely negative and are informed by the heterosexist biases discussed earlier. Mostly, she is credited with a lack of originality in using the most common meter available in puritanical New England culture, and it is assumed that she was merely modeling her work on the devotional forms ingrained in her mind by her religious upbringing. The fact that she creates variations in the meter in almost every poem has been taken to indicate her shortcomings as a versifier. With this interpretation, she is placed in a no-win situation. She is considered a weak poet for not originating her own meter, as Whitman did, but when she does stray from it, she is considered weak for not being able to adhere to the given structure.

One of the more favorable interpretations of this metrical puzzle has been put forth by David Porter. In his essay "Devotional Form and the Constant Occasion for Irony" he argues, in part, that "The form also provides for an ingenious complexity arising from the persistent secularity of attitude and language in counterpoint to the devotional schema. Hymnody, that is, provides a constant occasion for irony."[4] In other words, Dickinson consistently creates a tension between her ostensible devotion, as indicated by her use of the hymn form, and the markedly nondevotional attitude of her content. She utilizes the tension thus created between content and form to convey an ironic attitude toward traditional religious beliefs. While I would credit this interpretation above most of the others available, I believe Porter does not go quite far enough in recognizing the utterly subversive nature of Dickinson's technique. For Dickinson is concerned with more than the occasional irony implicit in any breach of faith; rather, she is concerned with the larger, overriding situation of irony implicit in her self-created identity formed within the breach of dichotomous thinking.

In disrupting the metrical regularity of hymnody, she is disrupting not only the systemic expression of religious doctrine, but the very possibility of systemic regularity itself in regard to any epistemological stance. In relation to poetry, closed, closely measured forms indicate the belief in the possibility of closure, conclusion, and certainty in knowing. By consistently disrupting this form, Dickinson is breaking away from this epistemological assumption. In the words of poet and critic, Judith Johnson, Dickinson is taking the hymn meter as a spine to support her poem, but then proceeds to "break the meter's back."

I would argue that Dickinson inhabits the traditional form of poetry like a ghost. She enters the hymnodic form and disrupts it from the inside, defying the expectations built into the form, much as a poltergeist defies our daily expectations for an object to stay in its place. She uses that disruption of expectation to her advantage, creating a fissure in the house of faith/reason/identity through which the light of her poetic vision, the darkness of her insight can seep in. Furthermore, I would argue that her disruptive inhabitation of the confines of meter is analogous to her disruptive inhabitation of the confines of heterosexuality. She lurks within the circumference of acceptability, of the recognizable, but with a difference. Some call this sort of existence oddity. I call it queer.

The fact that Dickinson was an avid reviser of her work, as is evidenced by the existence of multiple manuscript versions of single poems, attests to the level of awareness and linguistic skill she possessed in creating her variations. Given her extreme precision of word choice and syntactical construction in undertaking these revisions, it is highly unlikely that her metrical variations were not intentional. If she had wanted to adhere closely to the prescribed meter, she was quite capable as a versifier to do so. I believe she consistently disrupted the metrical norm in order to indicate her resistance to the epistemological norms of her and our culture. In the poem discussed above, for example (I'm ceded—I've stopped being Theirs—), she maintains the expected number of syllables per line (8-8-6-8-8-6), except that her first stanza contains seven, not the expected six, lines. This excess of line number coincides with her desire to exceed the limitations of name and identity imposed on her.

Part of what enables her to include this excess is her rejection of a regular rhyme scheme. Although she is ostensibly following one of the acceptable variations of the hymn form (aside from the "extra" line), she gives us only one perfect rhyme throughout all three stanzas: Erect/reject. If one accepts the theory that a similarity in sound (rhyming) implies a similarity or compatibility of meaning, then this particular rhyme can be seen functioning as a joke.

But jokes aside, throughout the poem, her main rhyming technique is slant-rhyme, and even this can be detected only through taking extreme liberties in pronunciation, by a particularly imaginative ear. In the first stanza, now/too and Dolls/spools could be forced into a rhyming relation, and in the second stanza, we can find a slight similarity in sound within the pairs choice/Grace, name/Diadem, dropped/up. Finally, in the third stanza we can link first/breast, Queen/Crown, and the perfect rhyme Erect/reject. Indeed, that would make this stanza the most "regular" of the three, since all of the lines can be paired, and one of these pairings is indisputable. However, the "regularity" of the third stanza is still odd in that it comes so late in the poem. Typically, a poet who employs slant-rhyme does so in a variant relation to a rhyme scheme already established much earlier in the poem. For example, as William Butler Yeats does in his use of the ottava rima, the tendency of rhyme is established in the early stanzas of the poem, so that we have a pattern by which variations can be recognized as still relevant to the norm. In Dickinson's case, however, she eschews the establishment of a "normal" scheme early on, where her off-rhymes would be recognizable as minor deviations. If anything, the "norm" she establishes in this poem *is* deviation. The deviation from this scheme is the one perfect rhyme.

Emily Dickinson's use, or more precisely, abuse, of traditional metrical form and rhyme scheme is integral to the expression of her content. In disrupting the boundaries of form, she is also subverting the metaphysical and epistemological implications that form carries with it. Much of her poetry involves as its subject the traditional formulating dichotomies of knowledge: heaven/earth, satiety/lack, life/death, conscious/unconscious, madness/reason, and so on. At the same time that she formulates her rebellion through the subversion of the "devotional" forms of verse, her poems subvert many of the usual distinctions of the dominant system of categorical dichotomies. The poem that illustrates this tendency most obviously is 435, "Much madness is divinest Sense—":

> Much madness is divinest Sense—
> To a discerning Eye—
> Much Sense—the starkest Madness—
> 'Tis the Majority
> In this, as All, prevail—
> Assent—and you are sane—
> Demur—you're straightway dangerous—
> And handled with a Chain—

Here, Dickinson is taking on one of the most fundamental categories of patriarchal epistemology and confounding the clarity of its distinctions. The distinction between madness and sense is crucial in maintaining an epistemological system founded on reason. The major underlying assumption behind the logic of reason is that our faith in its reality cannot be challenged. Thus, the distinction madness/sense not only determines what is permissible within the system of reason, but also formulates the ground for social control, to assure adherence to that belief system. In short, if you dissent with the majority opinion around this distinction, then you are considered "straightway dangerous—/And handled with a Chain—."

Once we recognize the centrality of this particular dichotomy to the entire Western cultural/social tradition, we can readily surmise the subversive impact of this "inversion" of values. Such an inversion is not an original notion and was especially prevalent in Dickinson's day. I am referring to the notion of poet as rebel, inspired by a divine "madness" of vision that ultimately reveals the Truth. And on the surface, that is about all one can say about the insight Dickinson expresses here. In the more straightforward reading, Emily Dickinson, with her poetic vision, is the "discerning Eye" that can detect the error of the prevalent, majority opinion. In short, she is claiming to hold an oppositional view: she sees sense in madness and madness in sense. But in claiming this, she, like her contemporaries, the Transcendentalists, would still be upholding the belief in the possibility of discerning Truth itself.

Upon closer examination of Dickinson's syntactical ambiguities, however, we can see that she does not rest her case with a request for special dispensation as a poet. She pushes her personal dissent into an indictment of the whole system of reason. The fifth line, "In this, as All, prevail" can be read as the prevalence of madness in society, and that this so-called sensible madness is the norm. The ambiguity rests in the word "this." If "this" is taken to refer directly to the statements in lines one and three, then she is saying that the majority opinion persistently upholds madness in the name of sense, and the notion of reason itself becomes impracticable. Thus, the "discerning Eye" does not belong to the poet/Dickinson but to the majority that upholds such a point of view. The fact that the word "Eye" is capitalized connotes a supreme being of some sort, whose vision is authoritative.

Neither of these readings is mutually exclusive; the poem can readily sustain both interpretations simultaneously. What Dickinson has created is a work of multiplicity, of difference that is not oppositional but can coexist. It is a both/and vision that is inclusive and expansive, not an either/or vision that must be exclusive in its search for a limited "Truth." The ambiguity that Dickinson strives to maintain in this, and all her poems, can in itself be seen as an indication of her "lesbian sensibility" or her "queer mind."

My sense of Dickinson as seriously playful can be best expressed through the image of the trickster.[5] In many cultures the trickster is an indispensable figure, and the form this figure may take is various and ever shifting. That variety and uncertainty is part of the trickster's nature. But the main function of the trickster is to remind us of our foolishness, our arrogance in believing in certainty, stability, and the immutability of "Truth." In *Another Mother Tongue*, Judy Grahn traces the ancient and historical connection between this figure and gay and lesbian existence. Cross-dressing and gender-blending are integral to the mystical crossing-over of boundaries attributed in most cultures to the trickster's shamanistic role. In our more repressive cultural epistemology, we allow this "extravagance" only to the poet, composer, and artist. While these are severely underrated and curtailed versions of the trickster, it does attest to the necessity and persistence of this figure, even in the horrifically narrow-minded "age of reason and science."

In light of this historical insight, it is especially fitting and ironic that Dickinson often referred to herself as a "little gnome" and other such fanciful figures. For playfulness, with the serious intent of shaking our world at its foundations, is the most consistent attitude in her inconsistent bag of poetic tricks. We of course have no way of knowing if Dickinson consciously recognized the force of this trickster's tradition of otherness, but we do know that she quite consciously created for herself a persona—that of the eccentric and reclusive spinster. From behind this mask, she was able to evade the demands placed on her existence by the exigency of heterosexism, and thus to disrupt the smooth domination of phallocentric thinking in her poetics. Much of what has been troubling to critics about Dickinson, I would maintain, was fully intended by her to be so. She is not a morbid despairing old maid, but an exuberant, defiant, troublemaker. Dickinson the poltergeist haunts language, meaning, and form, turning things topsy-turvy everywhere she goes.

NOTES

1. For a concise discussion of this history of Dickinson criticism, see Alicia Ostriker, *Stealing the Language* (Boston: Beacon Press, 1986), 4-6.

2. Rich, "It Is the Lesbian in the Us..." in *On Lies, Secrets and Silences: Selected Prose, 1966-1978* (New York: W. W. Norton, 1979).

3. Throughout this chapter, Dickinson's poetry and the numbered references are from *The Complete Poems of Emily Dickinson,* ed. T. H. Johnson (Boston: Little, Brown, 1960).

4. Porter, *The Art of Emily Dickinson's Early Poetry* (Cambridge, Mass.: Harvard University Press, 1966), 55.

5. I am indebted to Ostriker for her discussion of duplicity as a poetic strategy in Dickinson (*Stealing the Language*, 37-43) and for the suggestiveness of her discussion on multiplicity (203), although Ostriker uses it in a different manner, referring to the use of "we" by women poets to speak of "both multiple interior selves and herself joined to other women." Also see Rachel Blau Du Plessis, "For the Etruscans," in *The New Feminist Criticism*, ed. Elaine Showalter (New York: Pantheon Books, 1985) for a discussion of multiplicity as a "both/and vision."

CHAPTER 2

Imagery and Invisibility: Amy Lowell and The Erotics of Particularity

Although she is largely ignored and forgotten today, during the span of her literary career, Amy Lowell (1874-1925) was a central figure in the newly developing modern poetry scene. While Dickinson steered clear of public scrutiny in her lifetime, Lowell began stirring up trouble and controversy practically from the moment she arrived on the literary scene. She was unafraid of public controversy and placed herself firmly in the midst of the poetic battles that were raging between both the public and the proponents of the new "vers libre," and among members of the modernist movement itself.

The only vestige of her personal power and influence over the birth of modernism in America which remains within the canon of patriarchal literary criticism today seems to be the anecdotally conveyed renunciation of imagism by Ezra Pound. Moving onto a theory of "vorticism," Pound denounced his previous literary affiliation as "Amygism." Most critics seem to accept his dismissal unquestioningly as an accurate critical assessment: if Pound says his movement has degenerated into frivolity through the arrival of inadequate, female versifiers, then it must be true. After all, isn't he the father of modernist poetics? As if by the rule of "Father knows best," it is assumed that, by dint of his "originary" powers, Pound was, and still is, entitled to the right of developmental control over modernism. The new poetics was *his* baby, sprung full-blown like Athena from his amazingly fertile and spacious head.

Of course, the concept of "origins" and "originality" gains significance only in a heterosexist patriarchal system. Under patriarchy, it is necessary to trace all origins to the fathers to ensure the unquestionable male right of possession, control, and ownership. The woman's role, as both muse and vessel, is to inspire the male subject to undertake the (pro)creative act, and to receive and reproduce passively the effluence he produces. In all cases, the originary power resides within the male.

Amy Lowell in her garden. Circa 1916. By permission of the Houghton Library, Harvard University.

Yet, even James Joyce has written that "Paternity is a legal fiction," and Freud himself, in search of the originary "primal scene" of sexual neurosis, eventually had to question the validity of the concept of a single, originary event. As he delved into his patients' psyches, all he could discover were screen memories, one fictionalized account after another, in infinite regress, like the peeled layers of an onion. And as any good poststructuralist can tell you today, we have no direct access to the origin of anything; all we have access to is a *story* of origins, based on an arbitrarily chosen starting point from which we can begin the telling of the tale.

As for the "origins" of imagism, in an early letter to Louis Untermeyer, Amy Lowell wrote that Pound

would have ruined the movement, important though it was, as he has ruined everything he has touched....The only thing I object to in your article is your saying it was under his leadership that "the Imagists became not only a group but a fighting protest." It was nothing of the sort. The Imagists during the year and a half in which he headed the movement were unknown and jeered at, when they were not absolutely ignored. It was not until I entered the arena and Ezra dropped out that Imagism had to be considered seriously....The name is his; the idea was widespread. But changing the whole public attitude from derision to consideration came from my work.[1]

We can never locate a single origin of a poetic movement, for changes in poetics, as with changes in belief systems, do not occur suddenly with a single stroke of inspired genius. Rather, such changes are the result of an entire *zeitgeist*, the product of an accumulation of influences and circumstances, some of which we can trace, others of which will be lost to us forever through the forgetfulness that is history. As Lowell claims in the quote above, the name of Imagisme (with the affected "e") was Pound's, but "the idea was widespread."

Thus, one of the strongest yet most fallacious assumptions of heterosexism that informs the writing of literary history is the issue of originality and its concomitant issue, influence. In regard to these twin issues, it is now apparent that men and women, constructed as they are in this culture, have quite distinct reactions. In *The Anxiety of Influence*, for example, Harold Bloom makes it quite clear that the male literary tradition is driven by so intense a desire for originality, that the poetic "ephebe" is willing to turn patricidal, killing off all traces of his derivatory status. And if influence must show, the mark of the truly strong poet (or critic?) is that he will succeed in making it appear that the influence runs backward, that is, that the precursor is derivative of *him*.

On the other hand, feminist critics from Virginia Woolf (in *A Room of One's Own*) to the more recent Sandra Gilbert and Susan Gubar, have insisted that women need and desire to claim their literary foremothers, that discovering a continuum of women poets is empowering and validating. By placing themselves in community with other (female) thinkers, women writers create for themselves a context that reassures them, contrary to the dictates of heterosexist patriarchy, that they are not singular freaks of nature. Rather, they are part of a continuum of women who resist the confines of patriarchal gender identity. Women writers,

particularly those who attempt to live without male support, actively seek out
their predecessors in order to strengthen themselves in the struggle to create in
the face of what Gilbert and Gubar call the "Anxiety of Authorship."[2] Always,
women living under patriarchy must combat the male monopoly on originary
power, the myth that men are the only ones with something worthwhile to say.

Among the early circumstances and influences in the development of
modernist poetics, as Gilbert and Gubar point out in *The War of the Words*, were
the dual forces of the feminist and the sexual revolutions. While Gilbert and
Gubar maintain in their thesis that much of the work of the male modernist
tradition was written in reaction to what was then portrayed as "the battle of the
sexes," they also assert that these movements were particularly enabling, either
directly or indirectly, for women writers. The shifting of social codes around
"femininity" is a prerequisite for a woman to attempt the pen. When the questioning of
sexual and gender identity occurs on a large scale, then the quiet, isolated rebellion of
a Dickinson can gain such momentum and force that we can witness a
movement. The world, or a tradition of poetics at least, will never be the same.

As with the development of modernism in general, the lesbian identity and
poetic achievement of Amy Lowell grew out of a confluence of social and
personal circumstances. Born into a prominent Boston family, the first enabling
circumstance of Amy Lowell's poetic career was her financial independence and
her indomitable sense of class privilege. Unlike most women throughout
history, Amy Lowell was not directly dependent on the economic support of a
husband, father, or brother. While it is certainly true that her family money
stems from the capitalist impulses of her male predecessors, she herself had
complete control over her inheritance, so that there were no male authorities in
her adult life who held the purse strings. Thus, Amy Lowell was not at the
mercy of ongoing male approval for her financial well-being.

Furthermore, Amy Lowell was free on another level from desire for male
approval, the sexual. As she progressed from adolescence into young adulthood,
she began to suffer from what was probably a glandular disorder, which resulted
in an uncontrollable condition of obesity. For women under heterosexism, the
"desire" for male sexual approval is often more subtle than economic factors as
a control mechanism, but equally forceful in its effects. But by the time Amy
Lowell had arrived with certainty at her literary vocation, she had ruled out
marriage and heterosexual desire from her prospects.

While the circumstance of this "freedom" from heterosexual constraints
was not fully her choice, once she accepted her destiny to remain a "spinster,"
she knew that she held much more autonomy than was available to most women
in her day. These two factors, financial independence and sexual autonomy, combined
with the confidence born of her privileged place in a family of wealthy and
illustrious men, enabled Amy Lowell to pursue her career and her
unconventional aesthetic attitudes vigorously and with impunity. Amy Lowell
could *afford* to place herself at the center of controversy, both personally and
financially.

The appearance of Lowell's first collection of poems, *A Dome of Many Colored Glass*, was rather uneventful. Highly derivative of the Keatsian strain of romantic poetry, it gained little notice from the literary establishment, and perhaps rightfully so. It was with her next volume, *Swordblades and Poppy Seeds,* that Lowell's career of experimental and highly controversial technique was launched. The poems in this volume were written after she had encountered the work of "H.D., Imagiste" in Harriet Monroe's new magazine, *Poetry.* Upon reading H.D., Lowell recognized not only a new, sparser, and freely cadenced poetics, but she also recognized in her female contemporary a successful enactment of exactly the sort of poetic effect Lowell herself was still struggling to achieve.

Subsequently, Lowell made two trips to London to meet H.D., Pound, and the other poets loosely affiliated with imagism, which, in actuality was less of an organized movement than a casual weekly gathering of poets interested in trying something new. It was after these two trips to London and the publication of her second book that Lowell fully committed herself to the promotion of the new poetics in America.

From the start, imagism faced many detractors. Lowell began the struggle to demonstrate its strengths and beauties, through advocacy in her critical works and anthologies, and through practice in her own writings and public readings.

Concurrent with her discovery of imagism, Lowell made another important discovery that was also to affect the rest of her life. She met and became "close companions" with Ada Dwyer Russell, a successful character actor. The attraction between these two women was apparently immediate and mutual. Not long after the initial meeting, Ada Russell moved into Amy Lowell's family estate, Sevenels, and became Amy's lover, friend, editor, and business associate. The relationship lasted throughout Amy Lowell's life.

During her lifetime, Lowell openly acknowledged the mutually supportive relationship that the two lesbians shared and frequently joked that a sign should be hung above the front door, reading "Russell and Lowell, Makers of Fine Poems." In the will read after her premature death at the age of 51, Lowell arranged for Ada Russell to live at Sevenels until her own death and provided a trust fund that lasted the rest of Ada's life. It was Ada Russell who brought out three posthumously published collections of Lowell's work, including the Pulitzer Prize-winning *What's O'Clock?*

From the start Amy Lowell was concerned with tracing a genealogy of modernist poetics. In 1915 she presented a lecture at the Round Table in New York, crediting Emily Dickinson as one of the major nineteenth-century precursors to modernism. This lecture was eventually developed into an essay that appears in her 1930 critical volume, *Poetry and Poets.*

What I find to be most significant here, beyond the fact that Lowell was virtually the first poet/critic to comprehend the strength of Dickinson's genius, is that in doing so, Lowell was in effect creating her own lesbian continuum of poetic influences. One can see the poetic torch of modernism being passed directly from Dickinson to H.D. to Amy Lowell. Lowell herself may not have been aware of the nonheterosexuality these women held in common, but it is telling that she did detect a common sensibility or aesthetic shared by the three. Lowell's concern with the role of influence and originality, of community and individuality among poets, was a theme that ran consistently through her critical writings and lectures, and was immortalized in her poem from 1922, "The Sisters":

> Taking us by and large, we're a queer lot
> We women who write poetry. And when you think
> How few of us there've been, it's queerer still.
> I wonder what it is that makes us do it....

When Amy Lowell wrote these opening lines to "The Sisters," the word "queer," as slang for lesbian or homosexual male, was just beginning to gain currency. There is no way of knowing whether or not Lowell was aware of this connotation, but for readers today it is amusing that this amazonian poet, unapologetically lesbian and modernist in her poetics, chose just this word to denote the difference she saw between women poets and "regular women." Even if Lowell was not referring directly to the sexual identities of her poetic "sisters," she did find that a certain unconventionality, a strangeness from the "norm" of heterosexually defined "femininity," marked the lives of her poetic predecessors, and that this mark of difference was what enabled them to be poets.

"The Sisters" is Amy Lowell's tribute to this sparse "queer lot" of women poets who preceded her. At the same time, it is a questioning of the poetic legacy these "sisters" have left behind them. After "dreaming" her way through visits with "Sapho," (sic) "Mrs. Browning," and "Emily," Lowell concludes, "Yet indeed it's true—/We are one family. And still my answer/ Will not be any one of yours, I see./ Well, never mind that now. Good night! Good night!"

While Virginia Woolf advised women writers that we must "think back through our mothers," it is important to note that Lowell refers to her literary forebears as "Sisters." In doing so, Lowell is establishing an intimacy without hierarchy, a familial simultaneity of existence. This is appropriate since she is seeking to establish not a linear genealogy but a poetic continuum. By looking into the enabling "queerness" of her literary predecessors, Lowell was enabling herself. Lowell is also aware of the multiplicity. Even as she realized that she could not write like her predecessors, nor would she want to, she is still able to embrace them as "family"; she sees their struggles and strategies for creation as various, yet also directly relevant to herself.

One of the main strategies employed by heterosexist culture to erase lesbian existence is to impose distorting stereotypes through its descriptions of women's lives. Thus, the depiction of Emily Dickinson as a mild-mannered, though eccentric, spinster-poet has served mainly to mask her active rebellion against patriarchal thinking. Rendering the rebelliousness of her poetic vision and practice as a mere side-effect of her personal idiosyncrasies, the "straight mind" sets up the conditions by which Dickinson can be accepted as odd, but relatively harmless, in her rejection of the dominant worldview. This perceived harmlessness is possible through an emphasis on her spinster's life and her presumed celibacy. In a worldview where heterosexuality represents the only option for female sexual activity, the category of the female celibate formulates one-half of a dichotomy, that of the sexually active and the sexually inactive (heterosexual) woman. At bottom, this dichotomous distinction is built on an assumption of a fundamental heterosexuality, which can either be acted on or abstained from. The figure of the spinster also carries its own cultural burden of gendered attributes, not least of which is a reputation for being mild-mannered, accompanied by a certain self-effacing meekness, the result of an unrelenting propensity for altruism. For a century, Emily Dickinson was seen as falling neatly into this category, as countless other independently minded women have been cast into this category and thereby neutralized politically.

As with any stereotypic role imposed for the purpose of trivialization, there is a minor range of identities within the category. Thus, the spinster category can include women who had some sort of reputation for being social do-gooders, as well as those represented as the shrewish meddlers. It is this latter end of the spectrum of heterosexist description of the "unattached female" on which Pound and other detractors based their assessment of Amy Lowell's presence on the modernist poetry scene.

Amy Lowell was a forceful personality; physically large and verbally outspoken, she was not a woman who would allow herself to be dismissed easily. Furthermore, she had the finances and the class-born confidence to back up her poetic endeavors. Yet, according to her biographer, Jean Gould, Lowell's public debut at a meeting of the Poetry Society in 1915 was met with jeers, taunts, and outrage; by some accounts, rotten fruit was flung at the poet.

Gould speculates that the source of the audience's outrage was twofold: the perceived licentiousness of Lowell's free verse meter and the subject matter itself, a reverie on her daily life, beginning with a poem entitled "The Bath." Not only was this considered a rather intimate, and thereby inappropriate, subject for poetry by the staid Poetry Society members, but the fact that it was an obese "spinster" reciting these observations made the performance seem laughable. Gould writes:

Part of the reason for the uncalled-for ruckus may have been that though the New Yorkers ...had heard of Amy Lowell, they had not seen her, and probably expected her to be a sylphlike, frail, nervewracked, intense creature instead of the amazonian chieftain who rose majestically to read what seemed at the time a shocking poem. Perhaps because of her very bulk the effect of it was almost as shocking as if she had actually appeared in her bathtub in public; the uproar was an unconscious tribute to her ability for making things "real" in her poetry.[3]

According to the standards of a worldview where sexuality comprises the only legitimate ground for female eroticism, if a woman is seen as abstaining from heterosexual activity, then she is considered asexual. The value of this dichotomy for maintaining a heterosexist worldview lies in its erasure of autonomous female sexual power; female eroticism is either aroused (and thereby controlled) by heterosexual activity, or it is nullified, by lack of heterosexual engagement. Given the "physical deformity" (Gould) of Lowell's obesity, the clearly erotic implications of Lowell's poem "The Bath" did more than shock the withering Victorian decorum of her audience: it ruptured the very fabric of their heterosexist and sexist assumptions. Here was a fat spinster, not only describing her morning ablutions but *delighting* in them. The poem begins and ends with a reference to the scent "of tulips and narcissus in the air." The mention of narcissus, especially in conjunction with the green and white pool of water which is her bath, implies a level of self-love that is deemed inappropriate for a presumably celibate (and dejected) spinster. Such love and erotic awareness of a woman for herself flies in the face of all the carefully constructed self-loathing central to a misogynist worldview.

By applying Adrienne Rich's concept of a continuum of lesbian existence, we can perceive women who choose "spinsterhood" as radically subversive in their resistance to the pressures of compulsory heterosexuality, thereby taking control of their own erotic powers. Once we refuse to see female sexual power as contingent on the presence of male sexuality for its existence, then we can begin to uncover and accept the previously hidden powers of the erotic as it informs the lives and works of "spinster" poets.

In her essay "Uses of the Erotic: The Erotic as Power," poet Audre Lorde discusses the ongoing presence of erotic power in all women's lives and names it as a "resource" that "we have been taught to suspect" because it has been "vilified, abused, and devalued within western society."[4] In order to recover this resource for our own uses, it almost goes without saying that we must first reclaim our understanding of the erotic from the distortions put on it in by a misogynist, patriarchal culture. Thus Lorde writes:

> The erotic has often been misnamed by men and used against women. It has been made into the confused, the trivial, the psychotic, the plasticized sensation. For this reason, we have often turned away from the exploration and consideration of the erotic as a source of power and information, confusing it with its opposite, the pornographic. But pornography is a direct denial of the power of the erotic, for it represents the suppression of true feeling. Pornography emphasizes sensation without feeling....When I speak of the erotic, then, I speak of it as an assertion of the life-force of women; of that creative energy empowered, the knowledge and use of which we are now reclaiming in our language, our history, our dancing, our loving, our work, our lives. (54-55)

While Lorde's articulation of this power is possible because of her location in a contemporary context of lesbian feminist community, the erotic resource itself is not a contemporary invention; rather, it is a strain running through women's lives and creative endeavors in all times. In particular, I would argue that the power of the erotic is a primary source of poetic power for most, if not all, women who write seriously. In modernist poetics in particular, I believe it was the power of the erotic that enabled so many women, particularly lesbian and otherwise nonheterosexual women, to place themselves in the vanguard of modernism, as it manifested itself in numerous movements and "schools" of aesthetic experimentation.

It is clear that the aesthetics and techniques of imagism provided a powerful vehicle for Amy Lowell's erotic vision. Like Pound, H.D., and others, Lowell was strongly influenced by oriental poetry. She, too, did translations (from the Japanese), and her lyrical style is modeled, in part, on the cool but detailed "objectism" of the haiku and similar forms. This is obvious in the first two sections of *Pictures of the Floating World*, which are subtitled "Lacquer Prints" and "Chinoiseries." While many of these poems are somewhat pretty and delicate in their construction, for the most part they are fairly shallow, dealing merely with the surface image, as in "Circumstance":

> Upon the maple leaves
> The dew shines red,
> But on the lotus blossom
> It has the pale transparence of tears.

All this changes, however, in the subsequent sections, particularly in the section of lyrical love poems addressed to or about Ada Dwyer Russell, subtitled "Planes of Personality: Two Speak Together." Here, the detached observation of surface detail signals an undercurrent of passionate emotion and eroticism, disguised yet explicitly drawn in the natural images Lowell creates. A good example is "The Weather-Cock Points South" in which the "word-painting" of a flower-bud is so erotically drawn that it can easily be seen to represent the female genitals, so that this descriptive exploration of the flower is transformed into a celebration of lesbian sexuality:

> I put your leaves aside,
> One by one:
> The stiff, broad outer leaves;
> The smaller ones,
> Pleasant to touch, veined with purple;
> The glazed inner leaves.
> One by one
> I parted you from your leaves,
> Until you stood up like a white flower
> Swaying softly in the evening wind.

Here is evidence of how the discipline of imagism taught Lowell to focus only on relevant detail and to use a nondiscursive language, one that relies on the sensory qualities of the experience. Through the precision of her word choice, Lowell achieves a vividness of expression that appeals to several senses: sight (broad, smaller, purple, etc.), touch (stiff, pleasant, glazed), and also an implication of sound (evening wind) and scent (white flower). Lowell is relying not only on the detail of image to convey a sensual experience, but also on the textured patterning of sound to suggest a deliberateness, but with delicacy, a tender caution. The alliteration and assonance, featuring soft consonants and short vowels (such as *s,z,p,w,n* and flat *a* of *part, small, pleasant*) add to this gentle tone. The repeated line "One by one" slows the pace considerably, as do the short but end-stopped lines. The repetition of "leaves" at or near the end of almost every other line indicates that while there is movement and action taking place here, it is slow and explorative, almost worshipful in tone.

The second stanza takes on a more overtly reverential tone:

> White flower,
> Flower of wax, of jade, of unstreaked agate;
> Flower with surfaces of ice,
> With shadows faintly crimson.
> Where in all the garden is there such a flower?
> The stars crowd through the lilac leaves
> To look at you.
> The low moon brightens you with silver.

Here, the litany of attributes serves as a kind of invocation, a reverential, ritualistic form of address, leading to the awe-stricken question, "Where in all the garden is there such a flower?" This question is an assertion of the "flower's" unchallenged beauty. In the last three lines, the "flower" gains a majesty and splendor that cause the stars and moon to gaze and even bow ("low moon") with wonder.

In the last stanza, Lowell gives the most definitive clue that this white flower may represent something else altogether by the assertion in the first line:

> This bud is more than the calyx.
> There is nothing to equal a white bud,
> Of no color, and of all,
> Burnished by moonlight,
> Thrust upon by a softly-swinging wind.

The color white used to describe the flower also becomes associated with the moon here, carried over from the word "silver" at the end of the previous stanza. This association is developed further as the "white bud/ Of no color, and of all," is "Burnished by moonlight."

Many feminist critics today, learning to "read" women's poetry as encoded celebrations and explorations of female sexuality in nonpatriarchal terms, have pointed out that some images predominate for this purpose: in addition to flowers, the moon and its cycles are used to signify female sexuality. While these images are rich with erotic possibilities, I don't quite believe that Lowell was interested in encoding the sexual message too deeply. If anything, it seems Lowell wants to be sure that the reader gets the sexual connotations of the poem by using the already heavily connotated words "Thrust upon" at the beginning of the last line. Lest the reader think this is the familiar heterosexual "thrust," however,

Lowell immediately contrasts the potential violence of this verb with the sonorant phrase "by a softly-swinging wind." This final phrase carries lesbian implications not only in its reversal of expectations, but also in that it echoes back to the first stanza, where the wind is the only agent of motion besides the speaker, "I." Thus, Amy Lowell, who often read her poetry in person, by dint of authorship, associates herself with the speaker, who in turn is associated within the poem with the wind, as agent of erotic caresses.

Like Dickinson's, much of Lowell's work draws on nature, and even more specifically, on garden imagery. On the surface, this approach can seem to fit safely within the confines of the cultural expectations of "female versifiers," and much of Lowell's poetry, like Dickinson's, can be misconstrued as pretty little nature poems. Paradoxically, nature images are the perfect vehicle of expression for both of these poets' visions. It is familiar and readily accessible for both poets, yet they see in it an expression of their "deviant" beliefs and loves.

Lowell's poetics of imagism, with its preponderance of garden imagery, combined with her love for Ada Russell, allowed her to write extremely erotic lesbian poetry. However, because of Lowell's physical size and demeanor and the cultural invisibility of her erotic sensibility, the power of her lesbianism as a creative force within her work in particular, and within modernism in general, has been largely disregarded. Being aware of this expectation of triviality, and the overlay of heterosexist assumptions placed on Lowell's erotic life, allows us to see how the vision of the "straight mind" can erase the significance of this lesbian work from its place in literary history.

There is further significance to the use of nature imagery in Lowell's overtly sexual lesbian poetics. Not unlike Dickinson's use of the hymn meter to offset her own cultural heresies, the juxtaposition of "natural" images with "unnatural" sexualities creates an ironic tension between these socially constructed polarities, which forces the distinctions to give way. By bringing these "oppositional" concepts together, not in conflict but in relation, the boundaries of this dichotomy begin to disintegrate. Thus, by thinking with a lesbian sensibility, she throws the logic of the heterosexist culture against itself, and creates a paradoxical legitimation for lesbian existence: if nature evidences these "unnatural" images of sexual expression, then the "unnatural" is perhaps more "natural" than we have been led to believe.

While Amy Lowell is best known for "imagist" poems and lyrical lesbian love poems in which the techniques of imagism assert their influence, she also experimented with other techniques, some of them largely of her own invention (as with her development of "polyphonic prose"), some of them adaptations of more "conventional" forms (ballads, blank verse) put to her own revisionary uses.

One such type of "conventional" poetry is the lengthy narrative, often written in dialect and based on tales from New England. Several of these poems are presented in her posthumously published *East Wind*. In them, Lowell's characters tend to be lonely, without hope, often driven to despair, violence, or suicidal acts. Many live in or near decaying, ruined houses, the state of the structures tending to reflect the state of the people who occupy them.

Prevalent in the New England story-telling tradition, superstition and evidence of supernatural events are central elements of these tales, which appeal to our sense of horror, mystery, and fascination with the unknown. At first glance, this sort of poetic endeavor on Lowell's part may appear to be an anomaly, or even a reactionary throwback to a lost time, but upon closer examination we can discover certain traits common to all her styles.

Lowell believed strongly in poetry as an essentially oral art, and she supported this belief by reading her work in public as often as possible, at times even accompanying her submissions to the publisher's, so that she could present them orally. In her many attempts to explain and defend the "cadenced verse" of the new "vers libre," Lowell elicited the "musical phrase," as did Pound, for artistic justification. But she also insisted that poetry has a long and respectable oral tradition and that the reason for abandoning the "beat of the metronome" in modern poetry resides in the fact that poems are meant to be spoken. Lowell saw the "auditory imagination" aroused in the listener to be at least as important as the visual imagination aroused through "imagism." Thus, even her "imagist" poems tend to utilize what she called the "return"—a motif or repetitive pattern of image, word sounds, or stressed beat; and we are to understand these repetitions as necessary for aural as well as visual effectiveness.

Thus, the New England ghost tale, coming out of a long oral tradition of "yarnspinning," is an apt subject for Lowell's poetic explorations, and the fact that she wrote these poems largely in dialect both reflects and reinforces her notion that poetry is primarily a spoken art.

While from a late-twentieth-century point of view these narrative poems may seem to reflect little technical innovation, it is important to remember that Lowell's emphasis on American themes, regions, and speech patterns, and her exploration of the American character align her work with many of her contemporaries, all of whom were viewed as quite experimental and unconventional at the time. Edward Arlington Robinson, Robert Frost, and even Gertrude Stein were all concerned with exploring the richness of the American idiom and its role in expressing the confusion and conflict of a people caught in a changing time.

Lowell is a strongly artful tale-teller, and she often employs an "outsider" narrator, who, like us, is confused, shocked, and dismayed with the utter loneliness and hopelessness of her characters' situations. This "outsider" point of view, combined with the choice of two "spinster" characters, makes "The Doll" a particularly interesting example, from a lesbian point of view. In this tale, the narrator is a concert pianist who has escaped the small-town trappings of South Norton, though she often returns for visits with two spinster sisters, Jane and Julia Perkins. Unlike other poems in *East Wind*, "The Doll" is not written in dialect, signifying the narrator's escape and subsequent difference from the town's permanent residents.

> For many years I've always ended up
> With the two Misses Perkins. They were a whiff
> Of eighteen-forty, and I rather liked
> To talk to them and then come back and play
> Debussy, and thank God I had read Freud;
> The contrast was as genial as curry.

Over the course of the poem, we discover that Miss Jane, who is bed-ridden, keeps a large doll propped up in a wing-backed chair, facing her bed. The speaker notes this, then dismisses it, until she returns after Miss Jane's death to find that Miss Julia has moved the doll, chair and all, to face the window with a view of the street. Julia explains:

> It was so dull for her after Jane died,
> I moved her here where she could see the street.
> It's very comforting to watch the passing,
> I think. I always find it so...

Shocked by the implications of insanity in this conviction, the narrator blanks out on the rest of the visit, remembering only that she returned home that evening,

> And stayed up half the night playing Stravinsky.
> I dreamt wax doll for three weeks afterwards,
> And I shall go to London this vacation.

We can attribute the narrator's shock in part to the recognition that even her knowledge of Freud has not enabled her to discern previously the insanity of the two sisters. Playing Stravinsky furiously can be seen as a symbolic exorcism of this horror, an overzealous assertion of her own modernity. The possibility of this insanity rattles her and strikes a little too close to the bone, as is evidenced in her decision not to return. For the doll, if perceived by the two old ladies as providing company, becomes interchangeable with the narrator herself, and it is this simulcra of life which the narrator, in her modernity, is struggling to escape. Through understatement and suggestiveness, rather than overt statement of theme, Lowell creates a powerful poem that is extremely disturbing in its implications, particularly for New England "spinsters."

The return to, or reclamation of, an oral tradition has many links for Lowell with her lesbian, modernist poetics. The strongest and most familiar version of an oral tradition available to Dickinson was the hymn meter, and in some ways Lowell's appropriation of the New England ghost story as a setting for the transformation of Puritanical repression into the creative experimentations of modernity can be seen as analogous to Dickinson's own reclamation (and transformation) of the hymn meter and the values it implies. In addition to marking a connection with an oral tradition of poetry, much of Lowell's further experimentation with form focussed on the possibilities offered by free verse to convey sensation and emotion, as well as a more liberal range of subjects.

It should be fairly obvious that free verse (or *vers libre*, as Lowell insisted on calling it) is a particularly liberating form for a lesbian poet speaking her piece in the fracas that was the birth of modernism. Free verse breaks from the constrictions of formal poetic diction, the sentimentality of the past, and the entire worldview which more traditional poetics support. The technique is consonant with unorthodox subjects and attitudes, and helps move poetry away from "bookishness," its purely "literary" status. With its emphasis on sensory experience conveyed through language, free verse becomes one of the modernist techniques most amenable to conveying a lesbian erotic sensibility.

Another technique developed by Lowell carries the sensual linguistic experiments of free verse and imagism a step further in disintegrating the bounds of traditional poetic form. "Polyphonic prose," Lowell explained, "permits the use of all the methods: cadence, rhyme, alliteration, and assonance, also perhaps true meter for a few minutes" (Gould, 143). Lowell utilized this technique, which is prose only in its arrangement on the page into paragraph form, for a variety of subjects, including her cycle "Spring Day," which began with her infamous poem, "The Bath." However, in my opinion, Lowell was most successful in her use of polyphonic prose when her subject was war. In *Can Grande's Castle*, Lowell's fourth poetry volume, polyphonic prose was the dominant technique employed throughout the work.

Deeply affected by the horrors of the First World War, as were many of her contemporaries, in *Can Grande's Castle* Lowell created an epic work that drew connections between historical events, such as Commodore Perry's opening up of the East to American imperialism, and the raging battles of her own day. But this theme of the horror and confusion of war was not new to Lowell; in *Men, Women and Ghosts*, her third volume, she explored the theme quite vividly through polyphonic prose in "The Bombardment." This poem depicts a city relentlessly under siege; beginning with the bombing of a cathedral, the poem shifts through many scenes of bombardment, including a frightened child's bedroom and the laboratory of a dedicated scientist. Each scene is punctuated by a resounding "Boom!," which conveys the violence and overwhelming volume of the attack.

The poem begins by juxtaposing the steady splash of a rainfall with the start of the bombardment. The contrast of sounds and textures between the two different sorts of "fallout" serves to heighten the sense of violence and destruction, as does the intertwining of people's lives and actions with the deadly chaos. For example, in the third "stanza," she describes a poet at work when the bombs begin to fall:

> It rustles at the window-pane, the smooth,
> streaming rain, and he is shut within its clash
> and murmur. Inside is his candle, his ink, his
> pen, and his dreams. He is thinking, and the

walls are pierced with beams of sunshine, slipping
through young green. A fountain tosses itself up
at the blue sky, and through the spattered water
in the basin he can see copper carp, lazily
floating among cold leaves. A wind-harp in cedar-
tree grieves and whispers, and words blow into his
flowers of fire, higher and higher. Boom! The
flame-flowers snap on their slender stems.
The fountain rears up in long broken spears of
disheveled water and flattens into the earth.
Boom! And there is only the room, the table, the
candle, and the sliding rain. Again, Boom!—
Boom!—Boom! He stuffs his fingers into his ears.
He sees corpses, and cries out in fright. Boom!
It is night, and they are shelling the city!
Boom! Boom!

Polyphonic prose, with its chaos of meter, as well as its versatility of language and image, is particularly well-suited for conveying the confusion and violence of war. And in this poem, the returning "Boom!" in each stanza works especially well when read aloud. In fact, at her first public performance of the piece, Lowell enlisted the aid of her friend Carl Engel to stand behind a screen with a bass drum to accompany her "Booms!," thus turning the piece into a multimedia performance piece. The reading was highly successful. Lowell herself described it as a veritable "holocaust of noise and terror" (Gould, 160-161). Therefore, in performance, Lowell carried her experimental polyphonic prose even further in its capabilities for blending genres and styles, and for crossing literary boundaries of formal expectations.

Thus, even in her poetry which was not explicitly lesbian in content, Lowell continued to write from a sensual relationship toward language. Her various attempts to cross boundaries of thought, genre, and style, whether through imagism, narratives, or polyphonic prose, were all marked by a certain erotic awareness of the world, which I would argue stems from the need to redefine poetry, the world, and her relation to both from a lesbian point of view. As Audre Lorde is careful to explain to us, the erotic, when liberated from it heterosexual and patriarchal confines, is a source of power in all of our endeavors, not just our sexual acts. Lorde writes:

Our erotic knowledge empowers us, becomes a lens through which we scrutinize all aspects of our existence, forcing us to evaluate those aspects honestly in terms of their relative meaning within our lives. And this is a grave responsibility, projected from within each of us, *not to settle for the convenient, the shoddy, the conventionally expected, nor the merely safe.* (57, italics added)

The power and uses of the erotic enabled Amy Lowell not only to transcribe vivid sensory experience into her poetry, but also to stand her ground in the poetry wars of her day. By that generation, at least, she was clearly acknowledged as one of modernism's leading generals.

NOTES

1. "A Memoir by Louis Untermeyer," in *The Complete Poetical Works of Amy Lowell* (Boston: Houghton Mifflin, 1955) xxiv. Also, the poetry of Lowell is quoted from this edition.

2. Gilbert and Gubar, *The Madwoman in the Attic* (New Haven, Conn.: Yale University Press, 1984).

3. Gould, *Amy: The World of Amy Lowell and the Imagist Movement* (New York: Dodd, Mead, 1975), 174.

4. Lorde, *Sister Outsider* (Trumansburg, N.Y.: Crossing Press, 1984), 53.

CHAPTER 3

"This shows it all": Gertrude Stein and the Reader's Role in the Creation of Significance

Next to Sappho, Gertrude Stein (1874-1946) is probably the most famous lesbian writer in recorded literary history. However, although the nature and duration of her relationship with Alice B. Toklas has long been common knowledge, until recently most Stein critics when considering her work have chosen either to disregard politely Stein's sexual "difference" or to act as if this "difference" in Stein really made her no different from other "men of genius": that she simply assumed the male role and acted out her relationship with Alice heterosexually, in the timeworn tradition of the great poet and his companion/servant/muse.

In either case, we can see heterosexist assumptions operating to erase the significance of lesbian existence in the creation of modern literature. The first approach simply ignores sexuality and gendered positions as relevant in reading Stein. This is a surprisingly "generous" move when we consider that the gender of the writer has been taken into account critically since the days of Plato and Aristotle. Yet with Stein, many critics seem to have been content to accept her as an honorary "man," in the generic, universal sense. Stein's inclusion within the canon of modernist poetry depends on a willingness to disregard her gender and her sexuality, except perhaps to note in passing that she is one of the few "female" participants in the category, "Significant Writers of the 20th century."[1]

The second approach, to acknowledge Stein's lesbian existence but recast it in bourgeois, heterosexual terms, helps bring her life, if not her work, into the realm of the "thinkable." Critics favorable to Stein attempt to render her life respectable in these terms, while those who insist on her lunacy find that her inability to be authentically heterosexual constitutes the source of great "anxiety" in both her writings and her life. Both of these positions assume a fundamental heterosexuality, which, even if it is somehow strayed from, is still the standard.

The idea that a lesbian is really a man trapped in a woman's body, is only one of several ways that the straight mind can acknowledge lesbian existence and yet still manage to dismiss it as culturally or epistemologically insignificant.

Gertrude Stein. 1937. By permission of the Yale Collection of American Literature, Beinecke Rare Book and Manuscript Library. Yale University.

By acknowledging a "difference" that is in fact the same, the straight mind, with its limited range of what is thinkable psychosexually, does not need to make any structural shifts in order to accommodate anything "other" than that which is already contained within the perameters of its dichotomies.

In more recent years, with the rise of feminist literary criticism and the increasingly visible lesbian and gay liberation movement, it has become more acceptable to discuss Stein's lesbianism as a relevant factor in any critical assessment of her life and work. One of the more popular strategies for reading Stein as lesbian is to insist that there is a Steinian code by which she can speak to Alice erotically, without drawing censure from her larger public.

Advocates of this hermeneutic approach often claim that although Stein's code is arbitrary, it can be cracked, and once we have our cribsheet filled in, we can readily interpret everything from her frequency of orgasm to her guilt complex at having failed heterosexually oriented familial expectations. While the motives for devising such an ingenious critical approach to Stein may be genuine in terms of accepting, even honoring, the lesbian behind the "man of genius," the major shortcoming of this method is that it rests on principles that are antithetical not only to Stein's approach to composition, but also to her articulation of a nonhierarchically based lesbian existence.[2]

Gertrude Stein was a relentless advocate of what she termed "democracy." While this particular term, along with its counterpart, "equality," have been perhaps irretrievably corrupted for us late-twentieth-century readers, conceptually, the ideas these terms represent are still quite fresh. In more contemporary terms, Stein's "democracy" translates into our grappling with the nonhierarchical, the nonpatriarchal, with new ways of thinking that embrace multiplicity.

Indeed, such a discourse is very strange to our patriarchally entrenched linguistic consciousness, and many readers have felt intimidated, or even threatened, by Stein's strange discourse. For example, her aversion to punctuation has been received with varying degrees of hostility and confusion, yet she avoided it because she found it to be too directive. As Judy Grahn says about Stein's use of (or lack of) commas, "She thought this was condescending to and undermining of the independence of mind of the reader."[3] By eschewing grammatical structuring, with its privileging of the noun-verb phrase and its insistence on temporal closure, Stein was extending this democratic attitude toward language itself.

To some extent, the hostility some readers have felt toward Stein's irreverent deconstruction of "meaning" and her abdication of the privileged position of knowing (authority) is understandable, in light of how much of our social order depends on such principles. Usually, the occurrence of certain expected structures constitutes its own sort of "code," which allows the reader certain shortcuts to comprehension. Without these structures in place, people tend to feel ungrounded, sensing that all their assumptions about reality and their place in it have been dislocated. In many ways, this is analogous to how lesbian existence is received under heterosexism. To acknowledge the presence and difference of lesbian existence, even unconsciously, is unsettling of the "comfort" provided by heterosexist structures.

On an unconscious level, then, the fact that Stein actually was a lesbian and not particularly secretive about it probably fed into the critical resistance toward accepting the challenge of her experiments. This resentment can sometimes take the form of feeling excluded, as if one were being left out of the joke.

We can see why some believe she was writing in a secret lovers' language to Alice. But if this were true, why would she bother to seek publication and to elicit responses from many readers, even of the unpublished manuscripts? While it is true that Alice was probably the first reader to take her seriously and the one to give her the most support most consistently (her brother Leo mocked her), there is no reason to presume she was writing only for Alice.

From the outset of her writing career, Gertrude Stein was outside the literary establishment. Trained in psychology and medicine, and subsequently living in Paris, she was an interloper in the field of American letters. The writing she produced, always composed of relatively simple words and phrases, drew directly from colloquial diction; Stein's use of a finite vocabulary eschewed the use of "literary" diction. Through a combination of repetition and variation, Stein found she could create emphasis and degrees of emotional intensity without relying heavily on adjectives and nouns to further her descriptions. In this way she could begin to move away from the categorizing tendencies of these particular parts of speech.

By abandoning nominalism, a staple of traditional literary poetics, Stein also severed her dependence on metaphor. If she felt any clarification was necessary, she would repeat her "meaning" (her original word choice) in a slightly different verbal context. In this way, she avoided drawing resemblances between two dissimilar beings, since doing so would have falsified the unique being of the person, place, or thing described. Stein was always acutely aware of the variety, the multiplicity of identity, of "being."

Thus, her writing, always in an American idiom, defies hermeneutic approaches in its repetitive, sparsely punctuated, and illogical form, yet manages to engage us through its effective use of sound and tone. This kind of writing is best read aloud, for it is then that we can fully appreciate the "insistence" for which she was aiming:

> They did then learn many ways to be gay and they
> were then being gay being quite regular in being
> gay, being gay and they were learning little
> things, little things in ways of being gay, they
> were very regular then, they were learning very
> many little things in ways of being gay, they were
> being gay and using these little things they were
> learning to have to be gay with regularly gay with
> then and they were gay the same amount they had
> been gay.[4]

While it is exceedingly popular to consider Stein a singular "genius" existing in isolation without connection to poetic predecessors, particularly other lesbian or even female predecessors, I see Stein as a direct descendant of Dickinson. In her linguistic experimentation, Stein, like Dickinson, often plays with the multiplicity of language: its ability for ambiguity, equivocation, and unstable meanings.

In both poets, we can witness a propensity for disrupting categorical distinctions, and therefore the "truths" they establish. Whereas Dickinson does leave just enough traditional structure in place to make interpretation feasible, Stein pushes her poetics of disruption into the realm of the rationally unrecognizable.

If Dickinson's poetics are like a ghost that haunts convention, displacing objects and expectations, then Stein's poetics are like a volcanic eruption, permeating and undermining structure and form on every level, from the "balanced completion" of the sentence to that of the paragraph, through genres, and ultimately addressing the larger assumptions of culture and tradition itself.

One such set of assumptions that Stein's writing undermines is the concept of literary language and form, and the need for critical interpretation. The passage quoted above, taken from "Miss Furr and Miss Skeene," is fairly self-evident in its content. Only if one is operating from a critical base that assumes the symbolic, that sense is concealed rather than revealed through language, can one be puzzled by the "meaning" of the passage. It's "about" two women who learn how to be gay and then do so "regularly." The "difficulty" in reading this passage comes only when a reader refuses the obvious and retreats to the familiarity of heterosexist assumption. Of course, Stein is playing with this propensity to think "straight" in her choice of the word "gay," which puns directly on the different, but not mutually exclusive, denotations accorded the word.

In "The There That Was and Was Not There," contemporary lesbian poet and theorist Judy Grahn writes: "For years I thought: 'She is difficult,' until one day it occurred to me to say it the other way: 'She is easy. I am difficult.'...Suppose it is not that she is veiled and obscure but that we, her readers, are. We are veiled by our judgments" (Grahn, 5).

Of course, the veil of heterosexism works to obscure the lesbian content of "Miss Furr and Miss Skeene," but the obscurity is not inherent in Stein's use of language. In a further example of this cultural obscurantism, many readers have taken the presence of "some dark and heavy men" as well as "some who were not so heavy and some who were not so dark" to imply that Helen Furr and Georgine Skeene had heterosexual liaisons. But just the fact that the two women knew and "sat with" some men does not mean they are not lesbian. Contrary to popular mythology, lesbians do not hate men and often have friendships as well as other relationships with a variety of men. And these men could, of course, be gay men. The fact that some of these men were "dark and heavy" (and some were not!) could contradict another heterosexist stereotype—that gay men tend to be pale and thin as well as lispy and limp-wristed. When Stein mentions these male associates of Helen and Georgine, she states, "They were regular then, they were gay then, they were where they wanted to be then, where it was gay to be then, they were regularly gay then."

In her personal life, Stein was not "in the closet." Anyone who came to visit her understood the nature of the relationship between Alice and herself. In fact, her overt lesbianism eventually became a source of great distress for Ernest Hemingway, who would have preferred her to be more closeted. There is little reason to assume she was closeted in her writing. In her subject matter, Stein tended to draw on the "actualities" around her—people, objects, and events she had known.

Yet, even as she drew on these "actualities," it is really the use of language itself and its interactions with consciousness that constitutes her main theme. Unlike her contemporaries the imagists, Stein's concern with consciousness led her to abandon any pretense of "objectivity." Hers is a writing of intersubjectivity— and the psychosexual aspect of her own subjectivity was decidedly lesbian.

One of the accusations hurled at Stein by her detractors is that her writing is solipsistic, self-occupied, and self-centered. Yet in her search for the "bottom nature" of her characters, for the "essence" of objects and foods, she was really seeking to discover and record the inner being, the consciousness of the world around her. Paradoxically, she realized, particularly in writing her first "poetry" cycle *Tender Buttons*, that the only access she could have to these other "inner beings" was through her own consciousness. Thus, she discarded the illusion of objective knowing and its concomitant poetics of "objective" description, and located her writing firmly within her own consciousness as it played in contemplation across the surface of its subject. This "self-centering," as Judy Grahn calls it, ironically, was not self-occupied, but was geared toward what she termed "listening."

Stein herself always considered her writing to be accessible to anyone who would listen. She believed strongly in the intelligence of her readers, and in publishing her writing, she was inviting her readers to listen alongside her to the inner being of the subject at hand, as well as to the play of her own consciousness in its encounter with her subject. Thus, the subjectivity in her writing is not solipsistic, but an extension of subjectivity from and to others, a layering of multiple subjectivities. In order to create this writing of intersubjectivity, she knew she had to forego any attempt at representationality. Not only would a poetics of resemblance compromise the unique inner being of her subject matter, but it would also burden her language with associations and meanings that would interfere with the immediate experience of "listening."

In this one aspect, at least, Gertrude Stein was not unlike many of her contemporaries, who were concerned with divesting the English language of its cultural baggage and reclaiming its poetic possibilities from an overwrought sentimentality. But while others were occupied with wresting new meanings from the language to express the radical sentiments of a new age, Stein went a step further, attempting to divest language from the burden of representationality itself.

In "Patriarchal Poetry," Stein explores the traditional role of linear sequence in the creation of "meaning." Rather than de*lineating* her comprehension of the way this discourse functions, however, Stein simply demonstrates her knowledge through parody:

> What is the difference between a fig and an
> apple. One comes before the other. What is the
> difference between a fig and an apple one comes
> before the other what is the difference between a
> fig and an apple one comes before the other.
> When they are here they are here too here too
>   they are here too. When they are here they are
> here too when they are here they are here too.
>   As out in it there.
>   As not out not out in it there as out in it out
> in it there as out in it there as not out in it
> there as out in as out in it as out in it there.
>   Next to next next to Saturday next to next next
> to Saturday next to next next to Saturday.
>   This shows it all.[5]

Patriarchal language, and by extension heterocentric thinking, depend on a categorical approach toward identity. In this passage, Stein demonstrates her understanding of how the concept of "difference" depends on a dichotomous distinction that hangs on the simple negative "not."

Typically, in this system of discourse, "not out" is equivalent to "in it." Yet, this is only part of the story. The initial passage, "What is the difference between a fig and an apple. One comes before the other" illustrates the role temporality plays in categorical concepts of identity. This temporal structure is usually maintained through the linear sequence of grammar. Thus, when she plays with the distinction between "out" and "in" without the guiding structure of grammatical subordination, Stein shows us that the distinction cannot hold through a simple dichotomous negation alone. Such a distinction must also exist in a larger structural context, one that privileges a certain notion of time as linear sequence.

Taken together, these combined elements of patriarchal poetry, definition through exclusion, and adherence to "proper" sequence, allow the arrogant and grandiose claim to complete knowledge: "This shows it all." At the same time, by parodying the certitude of such a technique, Stein herself is claiming to have uncovered something important about the way such a poetics defines a consciousness. Her playful traversal of linguistic boundaries has enabled Stein to reveal these boundaries at work in our consciousness. Thus, her writing also "shows it all."

In her explorations of linguistic structure in its relation to consciousness, Stein returned again and again to the problem of grammar. For it is here that we find the keystone to both linear and hierarchical thinking:

In Stein's work the linear plot inherent in English language sentences falls away. The noun is no longer the all-important main character surrounded by subservient modifiers and dependent articles and clauses, the verb is no longer a mounted hero riding into the sentence doing all the action, while the happy or tragic ending of objective clause waits in the wings with appropriate punctuation to lead us through the well-known plot to the inevitable end period.

She let the characters (which in some of her writing are parts of speech or numbers, not people or other creatures) spin out from their own internal natures as she let them happen from within themselves rather than placing them in an externally directed context. She discovered them as she uncovered them layer by layer through the rhythms of their speech or parts of speech, and the patterns of their daily lives, she listened to them as her eyes listened to Cezanne's intensity of color, carrying this idea of equality further to where everything in a given field is seen as equally vital, life is perceived as a dance in which every element contributes to every other. (Grahn, 11)

Throughout her career, Stein experimented with various ways to achieve this effect. As she herself has written, she took her initial cue from Cezanne, Matisse, Picasso, and other early modernist painters. Stein began converting words from bearers of meaning and identity into plastic entities, treating them in their purely sensory character. She did this by arranging them next to each other, setting up and exploring spatial and tactile relations among them rather than the more conventional syntactic, semantic, logical ones.

For the reader, these relations can only occur in the present moment, since they are unique to the text, yet do not depend on what precedes or follows in it. The absence of a linear syntax (on the level of the sentence) or a narrative progression (on the level of overall structure) strips the text of any temporal reference to anything else in the text.

Thus, in reading her text, we must inhabit the "continuous present" of the text at all times. Since this focus on language without the linear structure of past-present-future is so foreign to our typical ways of thinking through language, Stein brings to the forefront of our awareness the linguistic structures on which our thinking usually depends. Through what is absent, we become conscious of the role linguistic structures usually play in our creation of "meaning."

When the text frustrates our attempts to formulate a coherency of significance, we are made aware of the extent to which our "consciousness," as it is socially constructed through language, depends on the concepts of meaning and identity to hold it together. Any "meaning" that may arise from reading Stein's text stems from the confluence of linguistic habit with the reader's subjectivity, which includes personal experience, outside knowledge, and leaps of the imagination, all interacting within the context provided by the text itself.

Just as she sought to work nonhierarchically within the linguistic field of her writings, Stein also sought to establish a nonhierarchical relation to her readers. Stein's poetics of intersubjectivity depends on the participation of the reader, with her culturally inculcated desire for meaning and the openness of her own consciousness as it plays across the text in search of this meaning.

By taking words from their expected context and placing them outside the confines of typical grammatical structure, Stein is creating a linguistic space where words can be more flexible. Taken out of the clearly defined roles of a patriarchal discourse, they begin to resonate with their own potential, as the reader is thwarted in her attempt to determine the author's intent.

Since Stein is not interested in conveying any definitive "meaning" through her text, her writing is void of the patriarchal concept of the author's "intent."

Rather, Stein seeks only to convey the play of her consciousness through language. She is abdicating her "authority" over "meaning," thereby subverting a hierarchical power and creating a more "democratic" relationship to her reader.

In playing fiercely with the multiplicity of language, Stein breaks down the distinction between author and reader in the search for "meaning." The absence of exact meaning is for Stein a space she opens up into a broad vista of significance, which she invites the reader to step inside to experience together with her, in the only time the text allows, the continuous present. The fluidity of language use she achieves by foregoing the hierarchizing structures of grammar allows each word in the text to reverberate with possible significances, and the reader's participation is crucial in this process.

Even when Stein's work focuses on her relationship with Alice, she invites us to participate in her play of consciousness as its language dances across the page. In what is perhaps her "most lesbian" poem, "Lifting Belly," Stein calls her disruptive poetics of intersubjectivity into action, so that the reader is invited into a lesbian world, the world viewed through a lesbian consciousness.

It is clearly evident that Alice played an important part in Stein's life, art, and sense of personal identity. Early on, in her portrait of Melanctha, Stein observed that everyone has loving in them and that this loving is a central aspect of identity. Nearly ten years later, in "Lifting Belly," Stein chose to write about the significance of the particular kind of loving she and Alice shared, and to explore the effects this loving was having on her own sense of being.[6]

Written while Gertrude and Alice were staying in Majorca during the First World War, the poem centers on the daily life and conversation shared by the two lovers. Although Alice had already been living with Stein for about seven years, Leo had moved out of 27 Rue de Fleuris only the previous year. The time period in which "Lifting Belly" was written (1915-1917) constitutes what must have been a "honeymoon" period in their relationship. Thus, it is fitting that the poem Stein wrote during this period comprises her fullest linguistic exploration of her relationship with Alice.

The poem places the two women in relationship with each other, and with the world and people around them. As they converse on various subjects with varying degrees of seriousness and silliness, they return again and again to the title phrase, "Lifting Belly."

Grammatically, the phrase constantly shifts roles. It is an action, a person, an event, and more. While the phrase has an obvious sexual connotation, Stein places it in an wide array of contexts so that the words begin to multiply with significances never before imagined. Thereby she destabilizes and expands its "meaning." Everything the lovers discuss in the poem is discussed in relation to "Lifting Belly." "Lifting Belly" becomes the lens through which the lovers view and speak of the world. It is their lesbian consciousness:

> Lifting belly is an occasion. An occasion to
> please me. Oh yes. Mention it.

> Lifting belly is courteous.
> Lifting belly is hilarious, gay and favorable.
> Oh Yes it is.
> Indeed it is not a disappointment.
> Not to me.
> Lifting belly is such an incident. In one's life
> Lifting belly is such an incident in one's life.
> I don't mean to be reasonable.
> Shall I say thin.
> This makes me smile.
> Lifting belly is so kind.
> (*Yale*, 10)

It is fairly common knowledge among lesbians and gay men that the process of "coming out" involves more than simply acknowledging and deciding whether or not to act on one's sexual inclinations. Because the decision to "come out" is made in the context of a culture that is hostile, or at best indifferent, to nonheterosexual choosing, this "personal" decision affects our relationship with the culture at large.

Coming out necessarily entails a "difference of view," since to accept the dominant view would render our lesbianism "impossible." This difference of view has been described by Audre Lorde as an "erotic knowledge," a knowledge that "empowers us, becomes a lens through which we scrutinize all aspects of our existence."[7] In "Lifting Belly," Stein is both celebrating and exploring the power of this erotic knowing in her life. She wants to share with us, her readers, the effects of "such an incident in one's life."

> Lifting belly is such an experiment.
> We were thoroughly brilliant.
> If I were a postman I would deliver letters. We
> call them letter carriers.
> Lifting belly is so strong. And so judicious.
> Lifting belly is an exercise.
> Exercise is very good for me.
> Lifting belly necessarily pleases the latter.
> Lifting belly is necessary.
> Do believe me.
> Lifting belly quietly.
> It is very exciting.
> Stand.
> Why do you stand.
> Did you say you thought it would make any
> difference.
> Lifting belly is not so kind.
> Little places to sting.
> We used to play star spangled banner.
> Lifting belly is so near.
> Lifting belly is so dear.

Lifting belly all around.
Lifting belly makes a sound.
(*Yale*, 13-14)

In devising techniques that are decidedly unlike traditional "patriarchal poetry," Stein does not set out to describe her relationship with Alice for us; a descriptive voice would automatically cast the reader as an outsider to the relationship. Rather, she wants to draw us into the play of her lesbian consciousness. She does this by bringing us into the poem as active participants in the wordplay of the language. For, above all, "Lifting Belly" is playful.

As she explores the eroticism of vision she shares with Alice, Stein also explores and celebrates the language in its erotic possibilities. The poem abounds with rhymes, homonyms, and associational relations among words and phrases. Bristling with what today might be called *jouissance*, Stein's text is an energy field, and we are invited to dance within the charged atmosphere of instability and overdetermination of meaning.

This is the way I see it.
Lifting belly can you say it.
Lifting belly persuade me.
Lifting belly persuade me.
You'll find it very easy to sing to me.
What can you say.
Lifting belly set.
I can not pass a door.
You mean odor.
I smell sweetly.
So do you.
Lifting belly plainly.
Can you sing.
Can you sing for me.
Lifting belly settled.
Can you excuse money.
Lifting belly has a dress.
Lifting belly in a mess.
Lifting belly in order.
Complain I don't complain.
She is my sweetheart.
Why doesn't she resemble an other.
This I cannot say here.
Full of love and echoes. Lifting belly is full of love.
(*Yale*, 30-31)

While it may be tempting to read "Lifting Belly" as a "dialogue" between lovers, the text itself resists such a reading. One of the greatest hindrances to a dialogic approach is that the poem is devoid of quotation marks or any other clear differentiation of speakers. The effect of the absence of clear reference marks is similar to that of Dickinson's ambiguously referenced pronouns: in both poets, ambiguity allows for a richly evocative multiplicity of significance. To try to sort out which lines can be attributed to which lover is not only impossible, but undoes what Stein has accomplished. Throughout "Lifting Belly," she is not trying to exclude the reader, but to create a shared linguistic space.

Rather than struggling to reassert an order intentionally eschewed by Stein, the poem might be more fruitfully engaged by giving ourselves over to the text as it is written. While it is true that the poem conveys a sense of intimacy between the lovers, the lack of attributive punctuation works toward inviting the reader into this intimacy. We must bring our own consciousness, full of imagination and inventiveness, into the text.

We cannot stand outside the poem in judgment of its "meaning" or its structure; we must participate in the construction of its "meaning" or else it remains meaningless. "Lifting Belly" is about relationship, the relationship shared by Gertrude and Alice, and the difference their lesbianism made in their relationship to the world, their consciousness of the world, and the events around them. Through a complex strategy of presenting us with a "dialogue" lacking quotation marks, in which a continually repeated and redefined "subject" ("lifting belly") is discussed with a determinedly ambiguous reference to other subjects, Stein makes the reader a participant in the conversation rather than an eavesdropper. In this way, Stein draws her readers into a relationship with her lesbian loving and perceiving. She is inviting us into the continuum of lesbian existence.

> Lifting belly is so kind.
> Darling wifie is so good.
> Little husband would.
> Be as good.
> If he could.
> This was said.
> Now we know how to differ.
> From that.
> Certainly.
> Now we say.
> Little hubbie is good.
> Every Day.
> She did want a photograph.
> Lifting belly changed her mind.
>   Lifting belly changed her mind.
> Do I look fat.
> Do I look fat and thin.
> Blue eyes and windows.
> You mean Vera.
> Lifting belly can guess.
> Quickly.
> Lifting belly is so pleased.
> Lifting Belly seeks pleasure.
> And she finds it altogether.
> (*Yale*, 49)

In "Lifting Belly," Stein brings to the forefront the play of the signifier as it joyfully traverses the boundaries of logic and identificatory meaning. Just as Stein's nontraditional use of language allowed her to experiment with nonhierarchically based forms of expression, her lesbian connection with Alice allowed her to experiment with nonhierarchical forms of human relationships.

Throughout the poem, several "roles" are mentioned: baby, pussy, caesar, bunny, husband, wife, mother, man, bird. But the lack of quotation marks makes it impossible to know which of the lovers to attribute lines to, so that the ambiguity of the speaker's identity feeds into the ambiguity of the roles named. The taking on of sexual/gender roles in the poem is arbitrary and temporary. Stein is playing with our expectations for such roles to be stable and consistent, just as she disrupts our expectations in regard to the grammatical functions of words. By inviting the reader into her linguistic dance, she is inviting us to experience the playful construction of identity, as consciousness, sexuality, and language collide within the energy field that is her text.

> In the meantime listen to Miss Cheatham.
> In the midst of writing.
> In the midst of writing there is merriment.
> (*Yale*, 54)

NOTES

1. For an excellent historical overview of Stein criticism, see Michael J. Hoffman, *Critical Essays on Gertrude Stein* (Boston: G. K. Hall, 1986). Richard Bridgman, *Gertrude Stein in Pieces* (New York: Oxford University Press, 1970) and Shari Benstock, *Women of the Left Bank* (Austin: University of Texas Press, 1986) were indispensable to me in writing this chapter.

2. I am indebted to Benstock for her argument advocating a reassessment of this approach and for the suggestiveness of her own reading strategy, particularly as delineated in *Women of the Left Bank*, 158-193. For approaches that favor this "lesbian hermeneutics," see Bridgman, *Gertrude Stein in Pieces*; Elizabeth Fifer, *Rescued Readings: A Reconstruction of Gertrude Stein's Difficult Texts* (Detroit: Wayne State University Press, 1992); Sandra M. Gilbert and Susan Gubar, *No Man's Land, Volume 1* (New Haven, Conn.: Yale University Press, 1988); Lisa Ruddick, "A Rosy Charm: Gertrude Stein and the Repressed Feminine," in Hoffman, *Critical Essays*, 225-240; Cynthia Secor, "Gertrude Stein: The Complex Force of Her Femininity," in *Women, the Arts, and the 1920's in Paris and New York*, eds. Kenneth W. Wheeler and Virginia Lee Lussier (New Brunswick, N. J.: Rutgers University Press, 1982), 27-35; and Catherine R. Stimpson, "Gertrice/Altrude: Stein, Toklas, and the Paradox of the Happy Marriage," in *Mothering the Mind*, eds. Ruth Perry and Martine Watson Brownley (New York: Holmes and Meyer, 1984), "Gertrude Stein and the Transposition of Gender" in *The Poetics of Gender*, ed. Nancy K. Miller (New York: Columbia University Press, 1986), "The Mind, the Body, and Gertrude Stein," in *Critical Inquiry* 3, no. 3 (Spring 1977): 489-506, and "The Somagrams of Gertrude Stein" in *Poetics Today* 6, nos. 1-2 (1985): 67-80.

3. Judy Grahn, *Really Reading Gertrude Stein* (Freedom, Calif.: Crossing Press, 1989), 10.

4. *Selected Writings of Gertrude Stein*, ed. Carl Van Vechten (New York: Vintage Books, 1972), 566.

5 *The Yale Gertrude Stein*, ed. Richard Kostelanetz (New Haven, Conn.: Yale University Press, 1980), 128.

6. For an insightful and specifically lesbian reading of this poem, see Rebecca Mark's introduction to *Lifting Belly*, published in book form by Naiad Press, 1989.

7. Audre Lorde, *Sister Outsider* (Trumansburg, N. Y.: Crossing Press, 1984) 57.

CHAPTER 4

The Rhythms of Experience: Mina Loy and the Poetics of "Love"

Although Mina Loy (1882-1966) was not a lesbian, I believe that by placing her in the context of a continuum of lesbian existence, we may come to a clearer understanding of both her politics and her poetics of disruption. For, as Adrienne Rich states, a continuum of lesbian existence is not meant to imply simply that all women are lesbians. Rather, it is a conceptual tool that can allow us to see "the depth and breadth of woman identification and woman bonding that has run like a continuous though stifled theme through the heterosexual experience." Such a concept can add new insight to our reading of women's literary history as it moves us away from "a perspective of unexamined heterocentricity."[1] And it is precisely such a move, away from unexamined heterocentricity, which marks both the life and work of Mina Loy, one of modernism's greatest forgotten poets.

Born in London, Mina Gertrude Lowy was a young woman when modernism was young, and throughout her career her own personal and artistic development parallels the development of several strains of modernist thinking, ranging from decadence to dada, futurism to feminism. Among her contemporaries, she was considered to be a major innovator of modernist poetics. In 1926 Yvor Winters named Mina Loy, William Carlos Williams, and Marianne Moore as the three poets likely to assert the strongest influence over the "younger generation" of modernists.

Her creative versatility was summarized in part by a reporter for the *New York Evening Sun* who in 1917 set out in search of a likely candidate for his profile of the "Modern Woman." After visiting the haunts of New York City's "bohemian" crowd, he had compiled a list of several possible subjects to choose from, which included women as diverse as Margaret Anderson and Margaret Sanger, Jane Heap and the Baroness Elsa von Freytag Loringhoven. Ultimately, he chose Mina Loy as the best representative of this class:

Mina Loy. Photo by Stephen Haweis, ca 1909, Florence, Italy. Collection : Roger L. Conover. By permission of Roger L. Conover.

She can and does write free verse and hold the intuitional pause exactly the right length of time....She can and does paint lampshades and magazine covers. She can and does act, design her own stage and social costumes and then wear them as if she had a whole regiment of customers....Moreover she can tell why Futurism is and where it came from[2]

Although Mina Loy was celebrated in the mainstream press as the quintessential modern, and she was well known and respected within modernist circles in both Europe and America, her work is all but forgotten today, and her name has faded into obscurity. Until recently, it was nearly impossible to find any of her work still in print. A beautiful collection was published by the Jargon Society in 1982, in the centennial of her birth. Entitled *The Last Lunar Baedeker* and edited by Roger L. Conover, this text is the closest we have to a complete works, and it contains over 300 poems and several prose pieces. However, it has subsequently gone out of print. In addition to the problems of the availability of Loy's written work, biographical and historical information about her had been scant, and the book opens with a lengthy introduction that provides us with much useful and necessary information about her life.

Fortunately, this state of affairs has begun to change. Conover has recently brought out another, smaller, but more accurate collection entitled *The Lost Lunar Baedeker*. Simultaneously, Carolyn Burke's long-awaited biography, *Becoming Modern: The Life of Mina Loy,* was also published. Together, these two scholars performed an excellent service toward reestablishing Loy's centrality as a significant modernist poet.[3]

Virginia Kuoidis, in her book *Mina Loy, American Modernist Poet,* provides us with the only full-length critical study of Loy's work. The study focuses at length on Loy's ongoing concern with the poetic and intellectual exploration of what Kuoidis calls "The Female Self." Even the most cursory reading of Loy's work immediately reveals a preoccupation with the female point of view in relation to the major social institutions of heterosexuality: romantic love, sex, marriage, and economics. Loy's perspective is always a critical one. Kuoidis places these concerns of Loy at the beginning of her study and does not choose to gloss over Loy's overt feminism and the radical challenges to sexism Loy's poetry presents. While Loy's creativity was often spurred on by contact with significant movement men such as the decadents, the dadaists, and the futurists, most often she wrote in dialectical opposition to their beliefs, moving from a temporary acceptance of their theses into her own challenging antitheses, ending with a unique and idiosyncratic form of synthesis.

In her ongoing encounters with modernism's exploration of the interrelation of consciousness, language, and identity, Loy could never forget that gender played a crucial role in the ways these interrelations were to be understood. The popular press could treat the emergence of the "modern woman" fairly lightly, from the angle of the "human interest story." But for the women who were living this experience, forging a new sexual, intellectual, and social identity out of the chaos of modernism, the struggle for self-definition was a serious, difficult, and at times painful task.

Loy first entered the "modernist" world through her early training as an artist with Angelo Jank in Munich and Augustus John in London. This schooling enabled her to take a first step away from her conventional middle-class upbringing and exposed her to the art-for-art's sake attitudes of the decadents. Her first husband, Stephen Haweis, a fellow art student and a member of the British bourgeoisie, seemed to embody the decadent philosophy. As an artist, he quickly dropped out of sight, but Mabel Dodge once described him as "very *fin de siecle* and sad.

The couple settled first in Paris, where Loy's artistic talent was recognized by her admission to the prestigious Salon d'Automne. In an early gesture toward establishing an independent identity apart from either of the heterosexually founded structures of marriage or patrimony, Loy used the dual occasions of her marriage to Haweis and her first painting exhibition in Paris to name herself. In 1904 she took the name Mina Loy. As Loy said, "The name is an assumed one, adopted in a spirit of mockery in place of that one of the oldest and most distinguished families of England" (*LLB82*, lxiv).

In 1907 Haweis and Loy settled in Florence. Loy's first years there were marked by depression and ill-health, probably brought on by the difficulty and isolation of raising children, and an increasingly troubled marriage. She did continue to expand her circle of artistic acquaintances through her occasional visits to the villas of Lily and Isidor Braggiotti, and of Muriel and Paul Draper, both of which served as centers for the expatriate community living in Florence. Then, in 1910 she met and became friends with Mabel Dodge.

Of this time, Loy stressed her increasing sense of isolation brought on by the demands of motherhood, claiming: "My conceptions of life evolved while... stirring baby food on spirit lamps." She was living like a "hermit crab occasionally lured to expansiveness under Mabel Dodge's flowering trees" (*LLB82,* lxvi). Meanwhile, Stephen traveled widely for increasingly prolonged periods of time, which exacerbated not only her sense of isolation but also her financial difficulties. The problem of money was one that would be with her for the rest of her life.

Intellectually and artistically, if not economically, the year 1912 marked a turning point in Mina Loy's life. Perhaps because her children were now out of their infancies, or perhaps simply because she had grown tired of her "hermit-crab" existence, Loy began a period of increased contact with numerous artists, writers, and intellectuals of the time, a mixture of both native Europeans and expatriated Americans.

She received visits from Gertrude Stein, who, now separated from Leo, was vacationing in Italy with Alice B. Toklas. During one of these visits, Stein gave Loy and Haweis a manuscript copy of *The Making of Americans*. Given Stein's self-consciousness and uncertainty about her nascent method of "composition," this act of sharing indicates that Stein felt an affinity toward the young couple and a certain degree of personal trust.

While Stephen was not so harsh in his judgments about Stein's literary insight as her brother Leo had been, Stephen did not grasp the significance of her experiment as fully as she wished. Mina did. Clearly, Stein was impressed. Twenty-three years later, she recalls the incident in *The Autobiography of Alice B. Toklas*, telling us that Stephen wanted commas, but that "Mina Loy equally interested was able to understand without the commas. She has always been able to understand" (132).

It was also around this time that Loy met and became life-long friends with Carl Van Vechten, who soon became her literary agent. After Stephen left for a world cruise, Loy began to agitate for a divorce, for which she solicited Van Vechten's support, telling him that love is "the parasitism of the weak" (*LLB82*, lxvii).

It is only speculation on my part that the meetings with Stein had anything to do with this decision to leave her marriage, but I would venture to say that Loy must have been affected by Stein's presence as an independent woman who valued her art over the opinions of those close to her. Perhaps Loy was struck by Stein as a role model of an innovative, intellectual woman who could forget the ubiquitous craving for male approval. At any rate, it is certain that Stein was among the earliest and longest-lasting contacts Mina Loy maintained among prominent lesbians of the period. Loy was welcome at 27 Rue de Fleurus throughout the years, both as a guest and at times as a performer of her poems at Stein's weekly salon. In 1927 Natalie Barney invited Loy to give the introductory lecture on Stein at a meeting of Barney's Academie des Femmes prior to Stein's own presentation of her work at the salon. There is even some indication that Loy was partially responsible for Stein's appearance at the salon in the first place, since Stein was not necessarily on the friendliest terms with Barney and her circle, nor did she usually associate herself with "women artists" as a group. Loy, on the other hand, increasingly did. However, the most significant connection between Loy and Stein, and the basis of their ongoing friendship is the fact that both writers were centrally concerned with an exploration of human consciousness as it intersected with new forms of poetic and artistic expression.

Gertrude Stein

Curie
of the laboratory
of vocabulary
    she crushed
the tonnage
of consciousness
congealed to phrases
to extract
a radium of the word (94)

While it is clear from this tribute poem that Mina Loy did not imitate the technical innovations of Stein, it is also obvious that she understood the significance of Stein's experiments. Loy became a fierce advocate of the woman who more often than not inspired ferocity in her numerous detractors. Admittedly, this small poem, written as an epigram for an essay on Stein published in 1924 is not among Loy's most experimental works, but it is extremely well constructed in its precision of both word choice and meter.

The use of a concrete scientific vocabulary heightens the association of Stein with Marie Curie, another experimenting woman whose discoveries literally startled the public into a new consciousness of the construction of the mundane world. In its association of poetry with scientific research, Loy is implying that experiments in either field have equal social significance, in an age that would rather have focused on practical science than modernist creativity.

The sounds of the words themselves are hard-edged, with the violent activity of "crushed" setting off its own chain reaction of hard *c* and *t/d* sounds until the movement of sound in the poem finally comes to rest on the most basic particle of language and consciousness, the "word." While the harshness of the sound-chain underlines the antisentimental toughness of scientific jargon, it also subtly implies the antisentimental toughness of the chain, or continuum if you will, of "new women": Curie—Stein—Loy.

Like Gertrude Stein, Mina Loy was concerned with the interrelationships of consciousness, language, identity, and sexuality. Like Stein, Loy was interested primarily in pushing all of these areas of being into a new era, one in which the traditional ways of knowing would be supplanted and surpassed. And, like Stein, Loy drew from her knowledge of the visual arts a concrete notion of the word as medium, as a plastic entity that could be isolated and elevated for its own sake, manipulated not by the ancient associational baggage of meaning it may carry but by its placement in a new context.

Estranged from its familiar contexts, the word can be made to cast a new illumination into human consciousness. Careful juxtaposition with other words startles us into an abandonment of the familiar for the abandon of the recklessly new.

In 1913 Mina Loy's association with the Italian futurist movement came into full flower. As a seven-year resident of Florence she had, of course, previously encountered some of the futurist tenets as published in the manifesto and elsewhere, but it was not until 1913 that Loy became personally involved with any of the movement's members. That year she met F. T. Marinetti and Giovanni Papini, to whose vitality, both intellectually and sexually, she was at first drawn. Temporarily, at least, Mina Loy found a direct relevance to her own thinking in the futurist program of moving both consciousness and artistic expression out of the past and into the future.

Although her intense association with the futurists was rather short-lived, it was under their influence that she began to write for publication. In 1914 Loy published "Aphorisms on Futurism" in *Camera Work*, a publication that served both to introduce her to an even wider international circle of modernist creators and to create for her a reputation as the only female futurist to date.

In "Aphorisms," we can discern which of the futurist beliefs Loy found particularly credible. Exhorting her readers to "DIE in the Past /Live in the Future," Loy insists throughout that "THE Future is limitless—the past a trail of insidious reactions." For Loy, "appreciation" of past cultural accomplishments is a form of clinging to mediocrity and fear, and only serves to restrain consciousness from recognizing its own vitality in the present moment:

> THEREFORE you stand not only in abject servitude to your perceptive consciousness—
>
> BUT also to the mechanical re-actions of the subconsciousness, that rubbish heap of race-tradition—
>
> AND believing yourself to be free—your least conception is colored by the pigment of retrograde superstitions.
>
> HERE are the fallow-lands of mental spatiality that Futurism will clear—
>
> MAKING place for whatever you are brave enough, beautiful enough to draw out of the realized self.   (152)

Loy's version of the futurist vision is meant to be empowering to the individuals who can, if they are strong enough in their convictions, influence the changes to come by asserting their own artistic will: "NOT to be a cipher in your ambiente, /But to color your ambiente with your preferences." Contrary to the futurists' intent, this call for independent thinking allowed her the means to explore in language what had been previously overwritten by a phallocentric literary tradition.

What Mina Loy soon became "brave enough, beautiful enough" to draw out of her own "realized self" was a poetry that, in both form and content, presented a bold challenge to the dictates of bourgeois social and poetic convention—to an extent that exceeded even the "radical" intentions of her male futurist mentors. Published in the 1914 inaugural issue of *Trend*, Loy's "Parturition" is perhaps the first truly explicit poem written by a woman about giving birth. While it may be obvious that discussion of so-called deviant sexualities, sexualities that differ from the phallocentric, heterosexual "norm" (such as lesbianism) would have been a shock to the general public, placing woman's subjectivity as she experiences the exclusively female process of giving birth would have been an equal shock to the system of a gynophobic/phallocentric culture.

With this poem, Loy begins her exploration of consciousness, using a language of disruption to map the new territories through which she travels. But here, it is an exclusively female realm, and her language reflects the difference this makes. In "Parturition," Mina Loy has already shifted from the ostensibly generic "He" of the "Aphorisms" to a definitely female "I." Nor can there be an implied "we" for whom she is the spokesperson. From the very beginning, she is "I," profoundly alone in the agony of her experience:

Parturition

I am the centre
Of a circle of pain
Exceeding its boundaries in every direction

The business of the bland sun
Has no affair with me
In my congested cosmos of agony
From which there is no escape
On infinitely prolonged nerve-vibrations
Or in contraction
To the pinpoint nucleus of being

Locate an irritation   without
It is   within
                                        Within
It is without
The sensitized area
Is identical   with the extensity
Of intension

I am the false quantity
In the harmony of physiological potentiality
To which
Gaining self-control
I should be consonant
In time

Pain is no stronger than the resisting force
Pain calls up in me
The struggle is equal

The open window is full of a voice
A fashionable portrait-painter
Running up-stairs to a woman's apartment
Sings
      "All the girls are tid'ly did'ly
      All the girls are nice
      Whether they wear their hair in curls
      Or—"
At the back of the thoughts to which I permit crystallization
The conception   Brute
Why?
         The irresponsibility of the male
Leaves woman her superior Inferiority.
He is running up-stairs

I am climbing a distorted mountain of agony
Incidentally with the exhaustion of control
I reach the summit
And gradually subside into anticipation of
Repose

Which never comes.
For another mountain is growing up
Which   goaded by the unavoidable
I must traverse
Traversing myself

Something in the delirium of night-hours
Confuses while intensifying sensibility
Blurring spatial contours
So aiding elusion of the circumscribed
That the gurgling of a crucified wild beast
Comes from so far away
And the foam on the stretched muscles of a mouth
Is no part of myself
There is a climax in sensibility
When pain surpassing itself
Becomes Exotic
And the ego succeeds in unifying the positive and negative
    poles of sensation
Uniting the opposing and resisting forces
In lascivious revelation

Relaxation
Negation of myself as a unit
      Vacuum interlude
I should have been emptied of life
Giving life
For consciousness in crisis   races
Through the subliminal deposits of evolutionary processes
Have I not
Somewhere
Scrutinized
A dead white feathered moth
Laying eggs?
A moment
Being realization
Can
Vitalized by cosmic initiation
Furnish an adequate apology
For the objective
Agglomeration of activities
Of a life
LIFE
A leap with nature
Into the essence
Of unpredicted Maternity
Against my thigh
Touch of infinitesimal motion
Scarcely perceptible
Undulation
Warmth   moisture

Stir of incipient life
Precipitating into me
The contents of the universe
Mother I am
Identical
With infinite Maternity
   Indivisible
   Acutely
   I am absorbed
   Into
The was—is—ever—shall—be
Of cosmic reproductivity

Rises from the subconscious
Impression of a cat
With blind kittens
Among her legs
Same undulating life-stir
I am that cat

Rises from the subconscious
Impression of small animal carcass
Covered with blue-bottles
—Epicurean—
And through the insects
Waves that same undulation of living
Death
Life
I am knowing
All about
   Unfolding

The next morning
Each woman-of-the-people
Tip-toeing the red pile of the carpet
Doing hushed service
Each woman-of-the-people
Wearing a halo
A ludicrous little halo
Of which she is sublimely   unaware
I once heard in a church
—Man and woman God made them—
                    Thank God. (4-8)

In the 1917 *Sun* interview, Loy is quoted as having said:

If you are very frank with yourself and don't mind how ridiculous anything that comes to you may seem, you will have a chance of capturing the symbol of your direct reaction...the antique way to live and express life was to...say it according to the rules. But the modern flings herself at life and lets herself feel what she does feel then upon the very tick of the second she snatches the images of life that fly through the brain. (*LLB82*, xliv)

And this is precisely what she does in "Parturition." In both content and form she refuses to "say it according to the rules." In content she explores what has been deemed socially taboo in a culture intent on erasing female genitals, along with female experience

Technically, the poem reflects the influence of both the language experiments of Gertrude Stein and the dictates of the futurist technical manifesto. Loy also goes beyond the techniques learned from her mentors to suit her own poetic vision and needs. With this poem, Mina Loy becomes an innovator of techniques later attributed to e.e. cummings. Her use of typography as integral to the poetic structure makes the page a spatial, visual event as well as an aural one. Capitalization, spacing within a line to set rhythm, the narrow shape, with its use of frequent line breaks for emphasis and timing, rather than sole reliance on punctuation and traditional meters, are all techniques she developed so that she could capture "the symbol" of her own "direct reaction" as she conveys the experience of parturition.

Her contacts with Stein and among the futurists taught Loy to trust the immediacy of conscious perception and to recognize that it was the artists' task to record the dynamic movement of the mind as it interacted with the sensuous world. To accomplish this, we can witness Loy employing several techniques delineated in Marinetti's *Technical Manifesto of Futurist Literature.* Among these techniques was a willingness to rupture syntax, eliminate punctuation and conjunctive words, and create tensions and continuities through rapid juxtaposition (or "a chain of analogies" as Marinetti put it).[4] An emphasis on nouns and active, present-tense or infinitive verbs, rather than a more traditional reliance on the adjective and adverb is also advised by Marinetti, but also recalls for us the compositional techniques of Stein. All of these techniques are evident in "Parturition," though they are mingled with Loy's own variations and even rejections of some of the futurists' dictates.

Primary among these rejections is Loy's use of the "I," which, according to Marinetti should be eliminated altogether: "Destroy the *I* in literature: that is, all psychology... Be careful not to force human feelings onto matter" (Kouidis, 57). Loy's rejection of this tenet is obvious from the beginning: "I" is the first word of the poem, and its use is continued throughout. Loy's speaker asserts the centrality of her sense of self not only throughout the recorded experience of parturition, but also in the way this experience transforms her understanding of the workings of the universe.

Huge in her self-centeredness ("I am the centre /Of a circle of pain /Exceeding its boundaries in every direction"), her consciousness attains an all-encompassing magnitude ("In my congested cosmos of agony") from which she cannot escape. Through her heightened sense of awareness, she is completely outside the realm of mundane experience ("The business of the bland sun /Has no affair with me").

Located fully in her own immediate experience, Loy's speaker recognizes that there is no outside. This paradox of location is expressed through her repetitions of the words "within" and "without," which are no longer polar opposites but relations within her own consciousness ("...the extensity /Of intension"). Rhythmically, by balancing long lines against increasingly short lines, by use of spacing for a strong pause within a line, as well as by using such a key word as "contraction" in the ninth line, Loy manages to convey both the rhythm of labor, and the rhythmic movement of her consciousness caught in the flux of this moment of life.

Even as Loy's speaker is immersed in a visionary consciousness to which others are oblivious, her awareness is expansive enough to include knowledge of their ignorance: "The open window is full of a voice /A fashionable portrait-painter /Running up-stairs to a woman's apartment /Sings..." Ironically, the sexist banality of his song underlines the differences between the categorical genders (male and female) as they are enacted in daily life, even as her pain begins "Blurring spatial contours." As the night of labor wears on with its delirious agony, she experiences a unifying vision in which, on a cosmic level, oppositions collapse. At the end of the eighth stanza, Loy's speaker tells us of her insight:

> There is a climax in sensibility
> When pain surpassing itself
> Becomes Exotic
> And the ego succeeds in unifying the positive and negative
>   poles of sensation
> Uniting the opposing and resisting forces
> In lascivious revelation

The "lascivious revelation" brought on by the journey into pain unites or negates several "abstract" epistemologically based dichotomies: inside/outside, self/other, life/death. While her "consciousness in crisis   races," the speaker finds that each side of the dichotomy resembles its counterpart. In Stanza 11 she realizes that the "undulation of living" found in the motion of flies feeding on a carcass is identical to the "Stir of incipient life /Precipitating into me" of Stanza 9. At the end of the eleventh stanza, the speaker tells us:

> Death
> Life
> I am knowing
> All about
>   Unfolding

As with her stanzas on the dichotomy of socially constructed genders when she contemplates the "fashionable portrait-painter /Running upstairs," Loy's speaker also moves between the abstract and the concrete when she focuses, through a rapid juxtaposition of images, on the angel/animal dichotomy of female sexuality. In language that reflects her interest in psychoanalytic theory (in contradiction to Marinetti's admonition to abolish "all psychology"), Loy writes that her consciousness races "Through the subliminal deposits of evolutionary processes.

What Loy finds "Rises from the subconscious" are the animal images of "A dead white feathered moth /Laying eggs" or "...a cat /with blind kittens /Among her legs" or a "...small animal carcass /Covered with blue-bottles." But rather than debasing her, Loy's speaker finds that these images buried in her consciousness enable her to understand her current experience and serve to lift her into "The was—is—ever—shall—be /Of cosmic reproductivity. "

Paradoxically, her identification with the one side of the socially constructed polarity of womanhood, the animalistic breeder, leads directly into an experience of the other side, the divine mother. In a further irony, the speaker's self-centered absorption in being an "I" does not lock her into her own personal psychology, but allows her to be "absorbed" into unity with the cosmos.

Yet, in the final stanza, Loy makes it clear that the speaker's cosmic experience of motherhood is not to be confused with the religiously manufactured image of woman's divinity, which she describes as "Each woman-of-the-people /Wearing a halo /A ludicrous little halo /Of which she is sublimely unaware." In "Parturition" Loy manages to debunk the patriarchally constructed myths of holy motherhood without robbing herself of her sense of mystic wonder at the experience.

By appropriating the "negative" images of woman's animality, she empowers herself with wisdom gained through a "lascivious revelation." Loy knows that she must take on the double standards, cultural myths, and sexual taboos that have traditionally constructed the meaning of "woman" so she can get past "that rubbish heap of race-tradition—" to reach the "realized self."

For Mina Loy, modernism's break with the structure of tradition could only be realized if sexual politics were understood to be among the major undergirdings of that structure. In this, she was not unlike her contemporary, Virginia Woolf. Both women could see that the continued privileging of masculinity would undo any modernist attempts to restructure our modes of perception. Both women saw phallocentric thinking as the major stumbling block to all liberation struggles, whether they be sexual, economic, or literary, focused on the individual consciousness or the wider politics of a social order.

Thus, while Loy was initially attracted by the futurist call for the rejection of a sentimentalized romanticism and the development of a "new man" and a "new woman" who could exist in sexual equality, she soon became disillusioned with the futurist program, as it became increasingly clear to her that this "equality" would continue to privilege the male side of the heterosexual dichotomy. She discovered that the futurists' concept of sexual equality meant that women had the right, even the social obligation, to become more "masculine" and to forego any exploration of the radical potential of the "feminine.

Monique Wittig, a contemporary lesbian theorist, has written that: "gaining control of the production of children will mean much more than the mere control of the material means of this production: women will have to abstract themselves from the definition 'woman' which is imposed upon them" (*The Straight Mind*, 11).

"Parturition" reflects vividly Loy's supposition that liberation from ancient prejudices involves more than a simple change of laws, but must reach deeply into the structures of consciousness itself. In the closing lines,

> I once heard in a church
> —Man and woman God made them
> Thank God.

Loy's tone of sarcasm is strengthened by the fact that her previous description of the birth-giving process is so vivid and detailed. The concreteness of the experience, particularly in its painfulness, undermines any assertion that the woman was not consciously and actively "responsible" for the birth. Yet, ironically, it is by focusing on the concrete details of her experiences and thoughts throughout the childbirth event that Loy has successfully achieved such an "abstraction" of her self, away from the phallocentric culture's construction of the sexes.

Already by mid-year 1914, Loy was confiding to Mabel Dodge that although she was "in the throes of conversion to Futurism... I shall never convince myself—There is no hope in any system that combats 'le mal avec le mal'... and that is really Marinetti's philosophy" (*LLB82*, lxvii). Taking her own advice from the "Aphorisms," Loy knew that in order to create "the new form... that moulds consciousness to the necessary amplitude for holding it," the artist must be willing to believe in the perceptions of her own consciousness, even if these perceptions go against the philosophies of the futurists themselves.

As Mina Loy became increasingly frustrated with the futurist vision, her love affairs, and her marriage, she continued to expand her own vision of sexual liberation toward a rigorous critique of the dominant heterosexual paradigm. In 1915, she wrote to Mabel Dodge "What I feel now are feminist politics" (*LLB82*, lxviii). Unlike many feminists of the time, however, Mina Loy had little faith in political reform alone (the struggle for the vote was still raging in America and England).

There is an urgency in Loy's desire for radical change ("TODAY is the crisis in consciousness"). While "consciousness" may seem a rather abstract forum for effecting these changes, Loy clearly establishes a concrete link between consciousness and the fact that it is shaped by social convention. Social convention, as expressed through traditional poetic and artistic form is the first obstacle the futurist wants to "leap" over, even if such invention seems at first "a mere irritant." This concern with consciousness as a vehicle of radical social change is at the heart of the futurist, indeed almost all modernist, vision, and Mina Loy carried this belief into her feminist thinking.

As a poet and an artist, she believed her role was to help effect a change of consciousness, particularly in regard to attitudes toward sexuality. Mina Loy knew that she must take chances, both personally and poetically, to convey the emergence of a "new consciousness" in her work. For Loy, not unlike Gertrude Stein, knew that "IN pressing the material to derive its essence, matter becomes deformed." And at the same time, both women knew that the public might not like or understand it.[5]

Among her contemporaries, Mina Loy was considered an excellent but "difficult" poet. Ezra Pound coined the term *logopoeia* specifically so that he could label Mina Loy's poetic style, because the combination of her technique and content was so completely different from anything he had previously encountered. His neologism was meant to indicate that her emphasis was on ideas and subtleties of meaning conveyed through a precise word-choice rather than the visual image (phanopoeia) or the musical effect of language (melopoeia).

While Loy utilized an increasingly "cerebral" vocabulary to explore the tension and paradoxes between a specifically "female" selfhood and a "masculinist" intellectual tradition, Pound's descriptive term is also misleading. In the first place, the term *logopoeia* implies that this feature overrides the significance of image and cadence in Loy's work. Yet, one of the marks of Loy's poetic achievement is her linguistic playfulness, her sheer love of language as tactile, itself a sensual element of the world. Her skillful use of repetition, internal rhyme, punning, and other forms of wordplay is drawn directly from Stein. Evidencing her own background as a painter and visual designer, as well as the early influence of futurist techniques on her work, Loy's use of the concrete image figures prominently as both a starting point and an anchor for her explorations in consciousness.

Although Loy was highly intelligent and uniquely strong in her own peculiar leanings toward the erudite, I suspect that her "difficulty" stemmed less from her intellectual vocabulary than from her radical critique of heterosexuality, not only as it had been constructed traditionally, but also as the modernists themselves continued to perpetuate it. Hence, her contemporaries rushed to label her as "cerebral" not so much because her technique was inordinately "difficult," but because her content was difficult for her readers to hear.

Much of Loy's work focuses precisely on the economic situation of women, in conjunction with their sexuality and intellectual ability; many of Loy's best poems take marriage in particular as a focus of criticism. For Loy, not only was marriage an institution that served to define women and shape their existence, but its influence reached into the lives of all women and girls, whether or not they ever actually married.

Heterosexual marriage exceeds the boundaries of particular individual relationships as a form of sexual/social control in that the culturally constructed notion of women's sexual "purity" has been tied directly to the economic and psychological well-being of women generally. In an unpublished manuscript from 1914, "Feminist Manifesto," Loy calls for "the <u>unconditional</u> surgical <u>destruction of virginity</u> through-out the female population at puberty—" (155). According to Loy, "Virtue" is a "fictitious value" imposed on women (and in turn, upheld by women) which will prevent women from entering into a full "apprehension of Life" (154), hence limiting her participation in creating modernity. Loy writes in her manifesto that

> The desire for comfortable protection instead of an intelligent curiosity & courage in meeting & resisting the pressure of life sex or so-called love must be reduced to its initial element, honor, grief, sentimentality, pride, & consequently jealousy must be detached from it....
>
> Another great illusion that woman must use all her introsprective clear-sightedness & unbiassed bravery to destroy—for the sake of her self respect is the impurity of sex the realisation in defiance of superstition that there is nothing impure in sex—except in the mental attitude to it— ... (156)

Although Loy is undoubtedly more effective as a poet than a polemicist, her "Feminist Manifesto" is remarkable in its insistence on the interrelations among women's political and economic liberation, the liberation of consciousness, the liberation of "the word," and female sexual liberation. Very few modernist women were able to make such broad connections, and of those who did (again, Virginia Woolf comes to mind), Mina Loy seems to have been the first to do so in print.

She did worry briefly about the effects of her outspokenness on her personal well-being, confiding to Carl Van Vechten that she feared Stephen Haweis was decrying her work as scandalous among their friends. Clearly, however, she did not let this momentary fear of censure silence her. Given her acute understanding of social convention and its links to epistemological frameworks, she knew that she must continue to work against sexist and heterosexist social conventions if she were ever to come in contact with and articulate her "realized self." Again, Monique Wittig is useful here as a gloss to our comprehension of Loy's personal conviction of the necessity and urgency of undertaking a rigorous social/sexual/intellectual critique. Wittig writes:

the category of sex shapes the mind as well as the body since it controls all mental production. It grips our minds in such a way that we cannot think outside of it. That is why we must destroy it and start thinking beyond it if we want to start thinking at all, as we must destroy the sexes as a sociological reality if we want to start to exist. (8)

The categorical thinking that creates and forcefully maintains gender (or "sex" as Wittig calls it) as an epistemological straitjacket and "as a sociological reality" is precisely what Loy wants to deconstruct in another early poem, "Virgins Plus Curtains Minus Dots." Published in *Rogue* in 1915, the poem argues against romantic sentimentality, while simultaneously making the point that romance as it has been socially constructed serves only to mask the mathematical coldness of patriarchal attitudes toward marriage and sex. As the title indicates, the system of gender inequity is formulaic, void of any true connection with the actual feelings and thoughts of the women involved.

Virgins Plus Curtains Minus Dots

Latin Borghese

Houses hold virgins
The door's on the chain

'Plumb streets with hearts'
'Bore curtains with eyes'

Virgins   without dots
Stare   beyond probability

See the men pass
Their hats are not ours
We   take a walk
They are going somewhere
And they   may look everywhere
Men's eyes   look into things
Our eyes   look out

A great deal of ourselves
We offer to the mirror
Something less to the confessional
The rest   to Time
There is so much   Time
Everything is full of it
              Such a long time

Virgins may whisper
 'Transparent nightdresses made all of lace'
Virgins may squeak
'My dear   I should faint'
Flutter.....flutter....flutter....
....'And then   the man—'
Wasting our giggles
For we have no dots

We have been taught
Love is a god
White   with soft wings
              Nobody shouts
        Virgins for sale
Yet where are our coins
For buying a purchaser
Love is a god
        Marriage expensive
A secret well kept
Makes the noise of the world
Nature's arms spread wide
Making room for us

> Room for all of us
> Somebody who was never
>   a virgin
> Has bolted the door
> Put curtains at our windows
> See the men pass
> They   are going somewhere
>
> Fleshes like weeds
> Sprout in the light
> So much flesh in the world
>   Wanders at will
>
> Some   behind curtains
> Throbs to the night
> Bait   to the stars
> Spread it with gold
> And you carry it home
> Against your shirt front ·
> To   a shaded light
> With the door locked
> Against virgins who
> Might   scratch (21-23)

Loy's concern with the "the category of sex" as both a form of mental control and "sociological reality" is readily evident in this poem, beginning with the multiple significance of the opening imagery. As Virginia Kouidis has observed:

Underlying the poem's obvious social commentary is sexual imagery that leads to the avowedly "metaphysical" preoccupation of all Mina Loy's poetry. The house, a symbol of the human body and the feminine principal, is locked and curtained, signifying virginity. The hatted men can, of course, open and enter the house if they desire. They have freedom, choice, purpose, vitality and, most important, penetrating vision. Their eyes "look into" life, permitting them attainment of selfhood, of "infinity." The eyes of the virgins (the curtained windows of the house), however, "look out": an otherness awaiting someone's permission to live. (32)

Kouidis goes on to argue that "Woman in her extreme deprivation, denied the vision of her own physical reality, is emblematic of the blindness, in one form or another, that afflicts most of humanity"(32). While Kouidis is helpful in establishing the connections among social control, sexual control, and the construction of human consciousness, I believe Loy was striving for even more than an emblemization of the female plight as a symbol of cultural aporia. She is offering language, the possibility of vision united with speech, as a way of disrupting the status quo.

By the direct juxtaposition of different sources of speech throughout the poem, Loy manages a subtle shift in speakers, and with this shift comes a shift in tone, or attitude, and vision. As a poet who believed that linguistic experiment was one area by which a change in consciousness could be effected, Loy is striving to accomplish more toward destroying "the category of sex" than simply revealing its inequities. She is pushing us, through the collective voice of the virgins, to "start thinking beyond it," as Wittig advises.

We first encounter the virgins at a distance, through a cool, third-person observation that implies their imprisonment:

> Houses hold virgins
> The door's on the chain

Next, we overhear what is said about them by other outside observers, as indicated by the quotation marks:

> 'Plumb streets with hearts'
> 'Bore curtains with eyes'

Already, a duplicity is slipping into Loy's language here, as she chooses two very active and forceful verbs to describe the virgins' allegedly passive activities. In the next stanza, Loy returns to the original third-person voice, but again, she grants the virgins more agency than it would seem they have, for she not only has them look out at the evidence of unjust gender practices, but also allows them a power to

> Stare   beyond probability

This probability could be seen simply as the likelihood of marriage, but it could also be read as an ability to see beyond the confines of that arrangement as well.

As the unmarriageable virgins look out from their cloistered lives onto the vitality of the street teeming with (male-dominated) human activity, they rely on a language based on categorical gender distinctions, which is ready to hand, to express their observations. They utilize an us/them framework, which serves to emphasize the vast distance between their own lives and those of the men who, as "So much flesh in the world /Wanders at will. "

While it would seem at first glance that this speech pattern confirms the virgins' adherence to this belief system, Loy subtly tints the apparent directness of their speech with an undercurrent of ironic cynicism. In the sixth and seventh stanzas, Loy begins to blend the speakers' voices, so that in the seventh, we have the third-person observer voice mingling with what is assumed to be said by virgins by other outside observers.

Loy's use of the word "may" here implies not only what virgins *might* say, but also what they are permitted to say: words that reinforce the mystique of romanticized love. In the seventh stanza, Loy further mingles the speakers by allowing the virgins' first person plural to join in ("For we have no dots"). Throughout the poem, Loy is giving voice to the unspoken truths underlying romantic mythology ("Love is a god /   Marriage expensive"). At the same time, by allowing the collective voice of the virgins to be the vehicle for this articulation of the not-said, she is converting them from passionless and harmless victims to powerfully disruptive elements, the bearers of knowledge that is even more taboo than knowledge of traditional heterosexual activity.

While the title of the poem with its curt, mathematical formula implies not only the severe heartless economic regulation of these women's right to existence as sexual beings, it also can be heard as an advertising slogan, a plea, and an offering shouted on the street: VIRGINS PLUS CURTAINS MINUS DOTS (get them cheap). This point is, of course, reinforced when the virgins say what

> Nobody shouts
> Virgins for sale

This stanza is a pivotal point in the poem. The virgins begin to reveal what they really know from being in their situation, rather than simply parroting the lines expected of them in their formalized and cliched roles. What they have knowledge of is the potential power of female sexual autonomy:

> A secret well kept
> Makes the noise of the world
> Nature's arms spread wide
> Making room for us
> Room for all of us

This stanza is juxtaposed with another factual observation of their imprisonment by men. By now, the third-person observer voice is completely merged with the collective first-person voice of the virgins. The virgins' vision is one of fecundity and passion; the light that causes flesh to proliferate is perhaps not the light of the male principal out there in the street, but of their own knowledge of female erotic power.

Perhaps some virgins "Throbs to the night" and "Bait to the stars" not out of longing for the man of their dreams, but because they also recognize the fecundity and the vastness of dark and cosmic mysteries. Perhaps the virgins' knowledge, like that of the mother in "Parturition," exceeds the boundaries of dichotomous thinking, of light and dark, of gender categories, of looking in and looking out, and they attain this knowledge through their awareness of themselves as erotic beings.

Such an awareness is dangerous in a heterosexist culture. This is why the "secret well kept," the "light" of their knowledge must be dimmed "behind curtains," against a "shirt-front," in "a shaded light," should a virgin be captured by someone who can "Spread it with gold"— the gold of either economic currency or romantic mythologies.

As is often true of Mina Loy's poems, the final lines carry a mocking tone, a tone that establishes both the fact of her knowledge and her awareness that this knowledge contradicts and supersedes the false knowledge of conventional belief systems. In "Virgins Plus Curtains Minus Dots," Loy effects a reversal in

the last stanza which is unexpected enough to catapult us back to the image of
the opening stanza, but here the houses that hold the virgins, where "The door's on
the chain," are designed not so much to protect the virgins or preserve their virtue as
to protect men from the virgins, whom they fear.

> With the door locked
> Against virgins who
> Might   scratch

Fear of women's anger, at the economic, sexual, social, creative, and artistic
repression that constitutes the definition of their categorical existence; fear of
women gathering in groups, of speaking/thinking/acting together and in autonomy;
fear of women's sexual, erotic, spiritual, and intellectual energy: all these fears
constitute the underpinnings of patriarchally constructed gender categories. These
fears are the motivation behind the adherence to antiquated social conventions.

In a move typical for Loy, she makes fun of this fear and the belief system
constructed to protect it ("A secret well kept /Makes the noise of the world").
Her creation of a suspense-laden pause in the center of the last line, followed by
such a weak-sounding and stereotypically "female" threat, calls up the notion of
machismo in order to mock it. At the same time, the threat resonates as
genuinely dangerous, both because it is unexpected and because Loy lets it
dangle there, without punctuation and with the full impact of all the emotional,
rhythmic, poetic energy built up throughout the poem.

Loy's poetic critique of the paradigms of romantic love and marriage was
not limited to a critique of the values of conventional society alone. In subsequent
poems, Loy focuses on how these paradigms of heterosexism remained one of
the most persistent forms of oppression even within the so-called sexual
revolution of her day.

"Songs to Joannes," is a cycle of thirty-four "love poems" addressed to an
evidently futurist lover. The first four poems of this cycle were published as
"Love Songs" in the inaugural issue of *Others* in 1915. In 1917, the complete
cycle filled an entire issue of the magazine. The cycle comprises a powerful
critique of heterosexual love and romance as a textual creation of the phallocentric-
centric discourse, even as this discourse was being subjected to modernist
revisions. In the first poem, Loy inverts the usual conception of romance as the
great elevator of base feeling into an ennobling transcendence. In Loy's view,
romance in itself is debasing, and belief in it keeps one bound to a narrow and
constrictive consciousness:

from   I

> Spawn of Fantasies
> Silting the appraisable
> Pig Cupid   his rosy snout
> Rooting erotic garbage
> "Once upon a time"

Pulls a weed   white star-topped
Among wild oats   sown in mucous-membrane (53)

While these opening lines of the cycle may indicate Loy's encounter and agreement with the futurist credo of antisentimentalism, she questions the role she, as a female, will be cast in (or will cast herself in) while "Pig Cupid" sows his "wild oats" in the anatomically described "mucous-membrane" of the female body. She concludes this first poem with her suspicions:

These   are suspect places

I must live in my lantern
Trimming subliminal flicker
Virginal   to the bellows
Of Experience
                              Coloured   glass   (53)

The image of fragmentation (Coloured glass) with which she "ends" this first poem is both an ongoing theme and a symbol of her poetic technique enacted throughout the rest of the cycle. As Virginia Kouidis has pointed out in her study of the poem, the phrase "Coloured glass" is a kaleidoscopic image that Loy introduces early on, and the poem itself comprises a kaleidoscopic view of her romantic/sexual experiences. Arranged in a collage format, each poem deals with a fragment of her experience. It is through rough juxtaposition of seemingly disparate pieces that she presents the reader with a full view of her engagement with internalized forms of romanticism ("Trimming subliminal flicker") on the one hand and the sometimes crude antisentimentalism of the modernist male on the other.

The form Loy creates in order to accommodate and express the complexity of her vision deserves much more detailed attention than I can give to the work here. Throughout the cycle, Loy weaves a complex of images involving "symbolic colors...cosmological images (sun, moon, stars), time images (day, noon, dawn, midnight, clockwork), animal and biological images and terms, images of light, vision, vegetation, flight, deity, the house, and mechanization" (Kouidis, 63). The complex interrelation of these images recalls and expands on the complexity of Loy's notions of consciousness, language, identity, and sexuality found in "Parturition."

As in "Parturition," the speaker of "Songs to Joannes" seeks to rewrite the "book of love" in order to heighten consciousness and liberate it from the narrow strictures of conventional morality. In doing so, the scope of her consciousness can range freely and without reservation through the entire span of human existence, from mundane life on the street to the expansive mysteries of the human's place in the cosmos.

Even as she embarks on this futurist's deconstruction of romantic love as nothing more than a fantasy built around the physicality of sex, Loy's speaker of the "Songs to Joannes" can't help but wonder whether this deconstruction doesn't have vastly different implications for the male and female modernist. While for the female, such a deconstruction may involve a difficult reassessment of the ways in which romantic beliefs have been internalized and clung to as a false form of self-fulfillment, Loy's speaker is compelled to wonder whether some secret, well-hidden fear might underlie the male antisentimental attitude toward sex.

Perhaps attempting to undo the bonds of romanticized sentimentality through reconstructing sex in a more mechanical way results in a loss of passion that would convert sex too easily from the overwritten sentimentality of romance to a completely meaningless act of cosmic vapidity.

IX

When we lifted
Our eye-lids on Love
A cosmos
Of coloured voices
And laughing honey

And spermatozoa
At the core of Nothing
In the milk of the Moon (56)

Throughout the cycle of the "Songs to Joannes," Loy is walking a fine line in her exploration of a failed vision of a (modernist) love affair. On the one hand, she wants to join with her male counterpart in describing sex in new and potentially liberating ways. On the other hand, she is suspicious of the male's readiness to throw off any obligation to human feeling in his sexual encounters. The freedom from sentimentality he seeks may in fact prove to be nothing more than an expansion of the conventional double-standard that allows the male to carelessly sow his "wild oats" and ignore any interaction of human consciousnesses that may occur there:

from   XIII

Oh that's right
Keep away from me   Please give me a push
Don't let me understand you   Don't realise me
Or we might tumble together
Depersonalized
Identical
Into the terrific Nirvana
Me you — you — me (58)

In poem XIV of the cycle, Loy tries on the futurist vision of humans as machines caught in the mechanical workings of an indifferent universe:

No love or the other thing
Only the impact of lighted bodies
Knocking sparks off each other
In chaos (59)

Counterpoised to the potential emptiness of this vision, Loy cannot simply abstract herself away from the fecundity of Nature, even if Nature has been used in service to the metaphors of repressive romantic love.

from   XXII

Green things grow
Salads
For the cerebral
Forager's revival (61-62)

Even as the lovers' resist these images of meaningfulness in sex, they are still drawn to them:

XXVI

Shedding our petty pruderies
From slit eyes

We sidle up
To Nature
— — — that irate pornographist (63)

Ultimately, Loy's speaker finds her initial suspicions confirmed:

from   XXVII

The contents
Of our ephemeral conjunction
In aloofness from Much
Flowed to approachment of — — — —
NOTHING
There was a man and a woman
In the way (64)

She finds that her questioning of the futurist antiromantic agenda leads to her "Crucifixion" as "a busybody /Longing to interfere so /With the intimacies /Of your insolent isolation" (from XXXI). In the penultimate stanza, she identifies herself as

XXXIII

The prig of passion — — — —
To your professorial paucity

Proto-plasm was raving mad
Evolving us — — — (67)

Loy's conclusion here, of the unreasoning evolution of human consciousness out of the chaos of biology, flings us into her final stanza, only one line long:

XXXIV

Love — — — the preeminent litterateur (68)

As we have seen with other poems, Loy's final lines are often heavily ironic in their meaning and tone. Returning us to the beginning, where the gross "Pig Cupid" is the "Spawn of Fantasies," she has covered several attempts at disengaging from these romantic mythologies, only to understand in these final stanzas that in her attempt to expose romantic love as a creation of the phallocentric literary discourse, she herself has contributed to the use of "love" as a central topic for her own literary endeavors. Along with the irony of this self-reflexive interpretation, Loy is also implying that her futurist lover, presenting himself in his sexual and intellectual vitality, is actually positioning himself in the role traditionally held by "Love" in our cultural mythologies, and, as such, wants to take over as "the preeminent litterateur."

In another poem also published in 1917 in *Others*, "The Effectual Marriage," Loy examines her growing suspicions of the fundamental hypocrisy of the futurist advocacy for sex free of social taboo. "The Effectual Marriage" presents the reader with a thinly disguised autobiographical account of her relationship with Giovanni Papini. Although Loy didn't marry Papini (or any futurist), in real life, the poem depicts the relationship between "Gina" and "Miovanni" through a narration of their married life. One of the central suspicions voiced in the "Songs to Joannes" reappears here, where she tells us that

While Miovanni thought alone in the dark
Gina supposed that peeping   she might see
A round light   shining   where his mind was
She never opened the door
Fearing that this might blind her
Or even
That she should see   Nothing at all   (38)

This suspicion of a hollowness that is at the heart of the futurist "vision" is couched in a narrative description of married life that is virtually indistinguishable from those descriptions produced by conventional society, with rigid separation of the male and female into distinct gender roles, highly reminiscent of the idealized "separate spheres" of Victorian middle-class morality. In this futurist "marriage," Gina's realm of action is confined to the kitchen with its "Pots and pans" where "she cooked in them /All sorts of sialagogues"; meanwhile, Miovanni's realm is his library, from whence he conceives of women, not as "immaterial," but as

> ...an incipience   a correlative
> an instigation of the reaction of man
> From the palpable to the transcendent
> Mollescent irritant of his fantasy
> Gina has her use   Being useful (36)

By 1916, Loy was finished with "being useful" as the futurists' token female. Her treatment of futurism in her poetry became increasingly satirical, and in Florence she began doing antifuturist performances. One poem in particular, "Lions' Jaws," published in *The Little Review* in 1920, reflects on her involvement with the futurist movement. It concludes that her role was simply to be the "secret service buffoon to the Woman's Cause."

Still raising her children and in need of money, Loy began working in various forms of commercial art, hoping to sell in New York. By the time Loy reached New York in October, she was already well known to the local modernist community and was welcomed immediately into various inner circles, including Allan and Louise Norton's group which published *Rogue*, as well as Alfred Kreymborg's group which brought out *Others*. She played the lead, opposite William Carlos Williams, in Kreymborg's play *Lima Beans* for the Provincetown players, also helping with costume and set design.

By early 1917, one could say that Mina Loy had managed to take New York by storm. She was profiled in *The New York Evening Sun* as the exemplar of the "Modern Woman"; she was given an entire issue of *Others* for the complete cycle of thirty-four "Songs to Joannes"; she collaborated with Marcel Duchamp in publishing *The Blind Man* and *Rongwrong*, two significant, though short-lived, magazines dedicated to Dada. In April, one of her paintings was exhibited as part of the Society of Independent Artists Exhibition, the show that shook New York's art world by bringing modernism to America.

Even with her successes among the avant-garde, however, Loy was still desperate for money. She had left her children behind in Florence with a nurse, while she struggled toward commercial success and finalized her divorce from Stephen Haweis.

Unlike Amy Lowell, Natalie Barney, or Peggy Guggenheim, who could escape the economic oppression common to most women because of their unusual position as female heirs of great family wealth, Loy had no family fortune to back her in her artistic endeavors. Nor did she have the modest but consistent income of Gertrude Stein, or even the constricted but financially secure existence of Emily Dickinson. Having rejected the security of a conventional, middle-class life for the life of an artist, she could not fall back on her family, nor could she rely on Stephen and his clan for help.

After she finally obtained a divorce from Stephen Haweis, Loy did not turn to the conventional female strategy of seeking economic security through a well-chosen marriage. She was quite beautiful and considered "charming" by many of her contemporaries, desirable for both her witty and insightful conversation and her physical attributes. Thus, opportunities for such a conventional solution as marriage did exist. Perhaps the most famous of the suitors who could have offered her such economic aid was William Carlos Williams, who apparently developed a crush so serious that thirty years later his wife remarked on it.

When Loy did, in fact, marry a second time, her choice had nothing to do with economic security and everything to do with the life of the mind and the abhorrence of conventional social and artistic values. In January 1918 she married the poet-pugilist Arthur Cravan, a precocious dadaist who thumbed his nose not only at mainstream convention but also at what he saw as the pretension of the emerging modernist artistic world.

Their marriage was poverty-stricken, tragic, and brief. Loy and Cravan roamed through Mexico for almost a year, trying out various schemes to make money, including founding a boxing school that promptly folded. By November, they decided to sail to Europe; they were nearly starving, Mina was pregnant, and she needed to return to her children after an absence of two years. While testing the small boat he had purchased to take them to Buenos Aires, a stiff breeze caught the sail and swept the boat out of the harbor and into the open sea. Arthur Cravan was never seen again. Alone, Mina sailed first to Buenos Aires at the insistence of friends and eventually on to England where she gave birth to a daughter whom she named Fabi, after Cravan, whose true name was Fabian Lloyd. After a visit to Cravan's mother in the spring, Mina Loy returned to Florence where she remained for the next year. This was Loy's period of artistic and literary silence, from 1918 to the early part of 1920.

In March 1920, Loy returned to New York, partially because she had heard rumors of Cravan's return and she wanted to look for him, partially because she wanted to renew her literary and artistic contacts among New York's avant-garde. She never found Cravan, but the literary and artistic contacts she made at the time were significant and endured for years.

Among others, one friendship that proved particularly strong and enduring was with Djuna Barnes. During this return visit to New York, Loy again left her children behind in Florence, and in 1921, Stephen Haweis kidnapped their son, Giles. Although she returned to Florence, she never recovered him. Within two years her son died.

Meanwhile, Loy was still in need of money. Given that she abhorred the conventional solutions to her economic problems that were available, Loy chose to practice her art, devising various methods of making money by it over the course of the remaining forty-five years of her life, but always with only marginal success. What minor success she did attain was through her lampshade business, which was set up with the backing of Peggy Guggenheim. With her usual parsimonious generosity, Guggenheim thought the shop would "free" Loy economically so that she could pursue her artistic and literary career. Instead, the business left her little time for anything else, and although "successful," lasting for six years, it also left her tired and in debt.

Despite these difficulties, Loy resumed exhibiting her art in various galleries in America and published her first book, with Contact, *Lunar Baedecker* (sic). In addition to these activities, during the two-year period 1923-1925, Loy wrote and published her long work "Anglo-Mongrels and the Rose," which Jerome Rothenberg has described as "comparable to, & probably not chronologically behind, Pound's early *Cantos* & Eliot's *Waste Land*."[6] He adds that "her work by 1918 had taken on a largeness of theme & an energy of sound & image that few in her generation could match." It was during this time that Loy began associating more with the women than the men of the avant-garde, particularly at the salons of Gertrude Stein and Natalie Barney, where she was sometimes there as performer, sometimes as guest.

After her strong literary activity in the 1920s, Loy turned her attention more fully to the art world, though more often as agent than artist. In 1927, Loy's oldest daughter, Joella, married Julien Levy, who was to open a gallery in New York in 1931, showing primarily surrealist works obtained largely through Mina Loy's contacts. From 1930 to 1936, Loy worked for her son-in-law as his Paris representative. Apparently, she became almost wholly absorbed in the art world business. She published only two poems in *Pagany* during these years.

She did continue to write, although the central product of this period has only recently (1992) come into print. *Insel* is a novel that fictionalized the surrealist personality of a German painter, Richard Oelze, whom Loy apparently befriended and possibly saved from a drug addiction. While radically different in subject and genre from her poetic works, the novel is not unlike her poetry in that Loy attempts to enact the surrealist consciousness through her form as she explores her subject, much as the poetic forms she devised often reflected the change in consciousness which was her theme.

In 1936, with the Second World War already brewing in Europe, Mina Loy moved first to lower Manhattan, and then the Bowery, where she lived until 1953. Roger Conover, Loy's posthumous editor, has included over fifty poems from this period in *The Last Lunar Baedeker;* more remain only in manuscript versions and are yet to be published. Numerous plays and prose works produced both during this period and earlier ones remain out of print today. In addition, it was during these years that Loy began a new experiment with form and medium in her art, creating "constructions" out of found objects, which depicted scenes from the Bowery life around her.

Her poems from this period were dedicated to a theme similar to the theme of her art work, the imagined consciousness of "the angel-bum" (Kouidis). She employed this figure as an image through which she could pursue her ongoing concern with the interrelation between transcendence and physicality, consciousness and identity, which shifted now from the site of the female self to the site of destitution and poverty.

In these poems from her later years, Mina Loy moved from exploration of self to examination of others who, unlike herself, were anonymous in their tragedies. "The common tragedy is to have suffered/without having 'appeared'," she wrote in "Show Me a Saint Who Suffered" from 1962. No stranger herself to hardship, poverty, and tragedy, Loy could identify with the destitution of those she saw around her, seeing their struggle for beauty and vision pitched against the suffering and difficulty of life.

The outcast status of the Bowery bum was not far from the marginal existence she had sometimes experienced as female modernist, heterosexual but unsupported economically by its institutions. She had bartered against social convention for her sexual and artistic autonomy.

The theme of the outsider who does not want to play or "say it according to the rules," who has vision and a need to articulate it even if "the new form, for however great a period of time...may remain a mere irritant" ("Aphorisms"), is a common one for Loy. In "Apology of Genius," published in *Dial* in 1922, she wrote:

Ostracized as we are with God—
    The watchers of the civilized wastes
    reverse their signals on our track

    Lepers of the moon
    all magically diseased
    we come among you
    innocent
    of our luminous sores

    unknowing
    how perturbing lights
    our spirit
    on the passion of Man
    until you turn on us your smooth fools' faces
    like buttocks bared in aboriginal mockeries

    We are the sacerdotal clowns
    who feed upon the wind and stars
    and pulverous pastures of poverty

    Our wills are formed
    by curious disciplines
    beyond your laws

    You may give birth to us
    or marry us
    the chances of your flesh
    are not our destiny—

    The cuirass of the soul

still shines—
And we are unaware
if you confuse
such brief
corrosion with possession

In the raw caverns of the Increate
we forge the dusk of Chaos
to that imperious jewellery of the Universe
    —The Beautiful—

While to your eyes
    A delicate crop
of criminal mystic immortelles
stands to the censor's scythe. (77-78)

In a poem often taken as one of her best technical achievements, Loy speaks for the necessity of the visionary's outcast perspective, for it is by exploring consciousness outside the "common sense" of social convention and propriety that new vision is wrought, and new beauty is found in the "chaos" of the universe.

Typically, the poem is read as a defense of the (generic) modernist's status as outsider, as the only person strong enough to effect artistic and literary innovation in a culture bent toward comfort and complacency. While the poem may readily uphold this interpretation, we may also hear in it now the particular strength required of her as a female seeking intellectual and sexual autonomy in a heterosexist culture.

The "we" of her poem may represent the modernist artists, poets, and intellectuals presented as outsiders, who may "come among you" but still existing apart, "beyond your laws." But "we" may also include the sexual "deviant," the nonpatriarchally defined "female." Perceived as sick and lunatic ("Lepers of the moon") by the dominant culture, they see themselves as innocent and magically possessed. In fact, it is this difference in view that creates their "otherness" from the rest of the culture, and it is why they cannot partake in the heterosexually determined (birth, marriage) "chances of your flesh." Monique Wittig tells us that

we say yes to the social bond when we conform to the conventions and rules that were never formally enunciated but that nevertheless everybody knows and applies like magic....Outlaw and mad are the names for those who refuse to go by the rules and conventions, as well as for those who refuse to or cannot speak the common language. (39-40)

The futurist vision of undoing the repressive aspects of social hierarchy was built on the notion of sameness; if everyone conformed to the same utopian principles and goals, we would see the future as "it EXPLODES with *light.*" But from the beginning of her encounter with this particular version of modernism and with modernism more generally, Mina Loy could not forget her own difference from the masculinist norm that her peers wanted to assert as liberatory. By clinging to her difference, as a female, as an artist on a quest for vision, as an intellectual exploring new forms of consciousness, as a poet seeking new rhythms of experience, Loy forged her own path into the future, cutting as wide a swath through the social fabric as she could along the way.

NOTES

1. Rich, *Blood, Bread, and Poetry* (New York: W. W. Norton, 1986), 23- 24.

2. Anonymous, "Do You Strive to Capture the Symbols of Your Reactions?," *New York Evening Sun*, February 13, 1917, p. 10, cited by Roger L. Conover, ed. in his introduction to *The Last Lunar Baedeker* (Highlands: The Jargon Society, 1982), xliv.

3. *The Lost Lunar Baedeker: Poems of Mina Loy*, ed. Roger L. Conover (New York: Farrar, Straus & Giroux, 1996). Throughout this chapter, all poetry is cited from this edition of Loy's work, unless otherwise indicated. Carolyn Burke, *Becoming Modern: The Life of Mina Loy* (New York: Farrar, Straus & Giroux, 1996). While I have utilized Burke's text to corroborate and correct facts and dates, most of my biographically related citations are taken from Conover's Jargon Press edition, identified throughout as *LLB82*.

4. Cited in Virginia Kouidis, *Mina Loy: American Modernist Poet* (Baton Rouge, Louisiana State University Press, 1980), 57. I am indebted to Kouidis for her thorough discussion of futurism and Marinetti's theories.

5. Quotes are from Loy's "Aphorisms on Futurism. "

6. Jerome Rothenberg, *Revolution of the Word* (New York: Seabury Press, 1974), 57.

Djuna Barnes. *"Samois*, 1925."* Papers of Djuna Barnes, Special Collection, University of Maryland at College Park Libraries. Reprinted with permission. Photo may have been taken by Thelma Wood.

CHAPTER 6

"A curious secret": H.D. and the Palimpsest of Sexual Identity

Although H.D.'s (1886-1961) writing career spanned nearly fifty years, during which time she wrote prolifically in a variety of genres, she is still best known for her early association with Ezra Pound and her role as the quintessential *imagiste* in a short-lived movement that came to have a long-term influence in modernist poetics. Pound's exhortation to "Make it new!" by applying imagist principles and Amy Lowell's persistent promotion of imagist works through the publication of several imagist anthologies, widened the influence of the new poetics far beyond the small circle of its originators. To this day, imagism has had a significant impact on the definitions and techniques of modernist poetics, effecting drastic changes in many readers' and writers' expectations of poetry. The subsequent poetics that developed among those poets originally associated with imagism are complicated and diverse, but the use of the original tenets—complete freedom of subject matter, attention to the exact word, and composition according to the cadence of the musical phrase—persists throughout a variety of later and longer works such as Pound's *Cantos*, Williams' *Paterson*, and H.D.'s *Trilogy*.

The story of "H.D., Imagiste" is fairly well-known, especially as it intersects with Pound's poetic adventures. Born in Bethlehem, Pennsylvania, and raised outside of Philadelphia, Hilda Doolittle met Ezra Pound when she was only 15, and he was a brash, eccentric, and very intellectual 16-year-old student at the University of Pennsylvania. The two nascent modernists began a poetic and romantic courtship that culminated, to the horror of Helen and Charles Doolittle, in the young couple's engagement in 1905. Pound subsequently returned to England, where H.D. later followed and arranged to stay on. It was during this year, 1912, that the now-famous meetings at the tearoom of the British Museum took place, when Pound, in a stubborn moment of masterful genius, penned the sobriquet "H.D., Imagiste" across the bottom of the page on which Hilda had typed "Hermes of the Ways" and a movement was born. To follow were publication of this and several other H.D. poems in Harriet Monroe's magazine *Poetry*, "Some Don'ts for Imagists" by Ezra Pound, and more poems in *Poetry* and *The Egoist* by Pound, H.D., F.S. Flint, Richard Aldington, and John Gould Fletcher. Next came the annual anthology of *Some Imagist Poets*,[1] which appeared from 1915 to 1917. It was the struggle for control over these volumes that caused Amy Lowell and Pound to argue viciously and publicly.

For H.D., this original association with imagism was both a blessing and a curse. On the one hand, it drew critical praise and widespread recognition of her talent practically from the moment she first published—certainly an enviable and encouraging situation for any beginning poet. On the other hand, this association with a particular "school" of poetics that lasted only a few years served to limit the scope of the critical acknowledgment that followed. While the centrality of Amy Lowell's role in the promotion of imagism has been minimized in the writing of modernist literary history, critics have tended to exaggerate the centrality of imagism to H.D.'s lengthy and various writing career. To be sure, H.D. has not been forgotten as the best of the *imagistes*; rather, other aspects of her poetics have been frequently obscured by critical assessments that rely on this association reductively. While it is true that the often-quoted tenets of imagism aptly describe some of her early poems, these tenets have never fully applied to all her early work, and over time, this description of her poetics has proved quite inadequate to the scope of her practice. Critics who have clung to this standard have often been confused and irritated by her longer poems, and even among those more sympathetic to her continued developments her poems remain resistant to explication.

As with the mythic association of H.D. with imagism, Hilda Doolittle's early connection to several well-known men of modernism has curtailed many critics' views of the sexual politics inherent in her poetics. While it has always been fairly well known that H.D. was bisexual, critics and biographers have tended to emphasize the significance of her heterosexual relationships to her poetic development. Often, her disappointments in these relationships have been cited as a source of neurotic instability. By focusing on the heterosexual aspects of her life and work, the questioning of her identity as a woman under that paradigm overshadows any questioning of her identity as a lesbian under a heterosexist regime. Certainly, this has been partially due to the lack of published materials relating directly to H.D.'s lesbian relationships, while information about her connections to Ezra Pound and Richard Aldington, among others, has been more widely available.[2] However, the recent publication of *HERmione* in 1981, and *Asphodel* and *Paint It Today* in 1992,[3] brings to light the significance H.D. gave to two lesbian relationships in her psychic and poetic development. Written in the 1920s, this trilogy of autobiographically based novels traces her emerging identity as a visionary poet and her strategies for negotiating the sexual politics of her day from a distinctly lesbian perspective.

Throughout *Paint It Today* (1921), *Asphodel* (1922), and *Her* (1927), H.D. portrays herself in continuous revolt against the mores and values of her day, particularly as they were imposed on young women of her class. Each novel focuses on some part of the period from 1905 to 1918, the years in which she was engaged in active struggle for attainment of an autonomous identity as a woman and a poet. These novels demonstrate that long before H.D. emerged in London as the best of the *imagistes*, she was already concerned with the possibility of attaining and articulating visionary insight, and this possibility was revealed to her through the sexual awakening of her first lesbian relationship. H.D.'s pursuit of this relationship and her struggle for autonomy brought her into immediate conflict with the social and epistemological order of heterosexism.

In *Paint It Today*, H.D. tells the story of this awakening and its subsequent social effects. Referring to the main character Midget, a thinly disguised representation of herself, H.D. writes that by recognizing her lesbian feelings for her friend Josepha (Frances Josepha Gregg in real life), Midget had "surprised a curious secret, surprised the secret or found the door to another world, another state of emotional life or being, a life of being that contained the past and the future" (12).

Contrary to the heterosexist mythologies of H.D.'s involvement with influential male modernists, such as her intermittent engagement to Ezra Pound, H.D. was not nearly so passively heterosexual in her relationships as many critics have maintained. Nor was she merely a neurotically unstable woman poet, overly dependent on the guidance and approval of male enablers. To be sure, Ezra Pound provided H.D. with her first serious literary education, as well as her first sexually and emotionally charged relationship. However, his was not the only or even the strongest influence on her early intellectual and emotional development. What the evidence of the novels indicates is the need for a complete critical reevaluation of H.D.'s bisexuality. Such a reevaluation must include a consideration of H.D.'s active engagement with a poetics of disruption, especially as it relates to the deconstruction of a binary system of gender identity. In *Paint It Today*, H.D. writes of her early concern with the role of sexuality and its relation to consciousness and visionary insight:

The fiancé had shown Midget what love might be or become if one, in desperation, should accept the shadow of an understanding for an understanding itself. Josepha had shown her or she had shown Josepha what love was or could be or become if the earth, by some incautious legerdemain, should be swept from beneath our feet; and we were left ungravitated between the stars.

I to not wish to belittle the Josepha incident. It colored Midget's life; it colors it still. (22)

For H.D., the discovery of the "curious secret" of lesbian sexuality brought with it a confirmation of something she had long suspected: that she could choose to explore "another state of emotional life or being," different from the seemingly preordained destiny of the dutiful daughters of the turn-of-the century American middleclass. The "door to another world" was a double discovery: that an alternative sexual/emotional life was possible for her, and an unusual intellectual/artistic life as well. This "door" revealed a world of alternate sexualities and of daemonic knowledge, of visionary insight, an awareness of "a life of being that contained the past and the future." The revelation and exploration of this other "state" of consciousness was the central theme of H.D.'s work, and the basis of her experiments in poetic technique from the early poems of *Sea Garden* (1916) through her last long work, *Helen in Egypt* (1954).

The notion of visionary power informing any artist is treated quite skeptically by our contemporary, technologically oriented culture, as it was in H.D.'s youth. Yet, despite the poet's apparent inutility in the twentieth century, poetry persists, and in certain quarters the notion of poetry's use as a means of achieving and expressing visionary insight remains vibrantly alive.

As with Gertrude Stein, H.D.'s strongest admirers have often been other poets. While the personalities and poetic techniques of these admirers are strangely diverse, all of them, whether early modernists, of the Black Mountain school, or postmodern feminist poets, have been engaged with the felt necessity to change the way we see the world through poetry. I believe it is this aspect of H.D.'s work, far more than her reputation as the best of the imagists, that keeps attracting her admirers. As Robert Duncan wrote in *The H.D. Book*, "Slight as the imagist poem might seem to be, it has also the charge of a vision—it is a card predicting a poetry."[4]

While many critics and readers of poetry may be reluctant to embrace a visionary role for the poet in general, it is particularly taboo under patriarchy to acknowledge this power in a woman. Hence, the figure of the poetess, the neurotically prolific female writer of small, emotion-laden lyrics, resides at the margins of literary history, as "a figure of disdain to male poets and of shame to women poets."[5]

Expanding on an argument made by numerous feminist scholars and critics, Duncan points to the misogyny and fear of female power behind the creation of this image. The poetess as figure of ridicule and scorn is maintained by patriarchal culture as a means of containment ─ ' ̗re. Since H.D. quite openly "is inspired reviving in the mear   ̗ne spirit of shaman magic and vision" (42), it is little wonder that   ̗dominantly male keepers of the literary canon would attempt to contain ̗ ̗r reputation within the confines of the imagist moment. Insofar as the system of patriarchy allows any of this visionary energy to sift into canonical consciousness, it is hardly ever allowed to transfer through a woman. The awesome power of the "Poetess as Creatrix," according to Duncan, evidences "a disturbing sex magic. Men live uneasily with or under the threat of genius in women" (43). In *Asphodel*, H.D. indicated that she was well aware of the dangers such male uneasiness posed. Recounting her visit in 1911 with Frances Gregg and her mother, Julia, to Rouen, the site of Joan of Arc's "crucifixion" (8), H.D. wrote:

And they had caught her. Caught her. Trapped her with her armour and her panache and her glory and her pride. They had trapped her, a girl who was a boy and they would always do that. They would always trap them, bash their heads, like broken flowers from the stalks, break them for seeing things, having "visions" like she did and like Fayne Rabb. This was the warning. Joan of Arc (9).

Reading the poems from H.D.'s inaugural volume, *Sea Garden*, Eileen Gregory suggests that the disreputable figure of the poetess has overshadowed H.D.'s reputation even among her critical advocates. Initially, H.D.'s achievements as an imagist could be recognized only to the extent that these early poems affirm the supposedly limited talents of the poetess as a writer of brief, emotionally intense lyrics. More recent critics, wanting to expand H.D.'s reputation as a writer of intellectually and psychologically complicated longer works, have often treated her imagist accomplishments as a developmental stage, implying agreement with the assessment of imagism as a preliminary and rather weak achievement. Gregory suggests that even "this recovery of her stature is made in part out of an aversion to the specter of the Poetess, the limited lyricist....Thus the early poems have been admired in the past for the same reason that they have lately been ignored: they point to the limitation of the Poetess" (526-527).

Rather than continuing this aversion, Gregory proposes that we rehabilitate the Poetess as a figure of visionary and poetic power: "Just as feminists have reclaimed such marginal figures as the Spinster and the Witch, so we need now to recover proper awe for the Poetess" (527). In this, Gregory is following Duncan's suggestion that this figure represents "the genius of woman that men would propitiate or exorcise. The Poetess was an enormous persona like the hieratic figures of women in the major arcana of the Tarot" (39). In relation to H.D. in particular, the reclamation of a figure of daemonic energy and mystical understandings engaged in the writing of texts is especially useful, since this figure approximates the role she understood herself to be fulfilling. As Gregory insists, and the evidence of the recently published novels confirms, "From the beginning of her career, H.D. indeed takes the Poetess as a guide. As a presence in her poetry, however, this figure suggests not limitation but scope, not shallowness but depth of erotic experience, not shamefulness and cowardice but deliberate courage" (527).

H.D.'s involvement with ancient mythologies and landscapes, especially those of Greece, has been the subject of much commentary. At times, this classicism has been seen as an exercise in escapism, an attempt to create a cold, harsh, and emotionally/sexually austere world to which she can retreat from the heat and turmoil of sensation and passion. Or, conversely, H.D.'s classicism has been seen as obscurantist, fraught with sexual/emotional tension from which she has stripped all personal details, creating an elaborate screen to hide the full nature of her desire so that what emerges is a sense of concentrated energy and passion, chiseled to its ultimate intensity, barely restrained. What Gregory, Duncan, and other recent critics have done is open the door to another way of understanding H.D.'s fascination with ancient myths, personae, and locales.

By acknowledging H.D.'s consciously chosen commitment to the renewal of poetry in the service of vision, we can view her classicism not as an act of escapism or masking but as an act of empowerment. Rather than an evasion of contemporary reality or obscuring of personal identity, H.D.'s poetic explorations reflect an engaged response to the stifling conventionality and nihilistic despair of her times, and an honest search for the emotional, psychological, and spiritual truths of personal identity. H.D.'s concern with classical and mythological subjects was driven by the desire to reclaim and enact her ancestral office, the Poetess. And here it is important to remember that it was her involvement in lesbian sexuality that opened "the door to another world" of visionary possibilities. In the recovery of the Poetess as a hieratic figure, as with the Spinster and the Witch, we must not erase the queer sexuality of these figures, for the construction of alternate sexual identities is a significant aspect of their powers. As Robert Duncan remarks, the Poetess's power resides in her "disturbing sex magic."

When H.D., through her initiation into the world of lesbian sexuality "surprised a curious secret" of "a life of being that contained the past and the future," she stumbled upon an insight that would sustain her poetics for the rest of her life. H.D. drew from this discovery an understanding of the continuity of her own experience with ancient stories and with the modernist desire to influence the future. Eventually, she would articulate this understanding of temporal continuity, or perhaps more precisely, simultaneity, through her notion of the palimpsest. A palimpsest as a parchment from which writing has been partially erased to make room for another text is an apt metaphor for H.D.'s understanding of mythological processes.

One of the ongoing difficulties faced by the heterosexist regime is its necessary erasure of lesbian and gay existence throughout history. As with every coverup, there is seepage where the thing that was covered over leaks through. Despite centuries of omission, distortion, and outright destruction, the evidence that lesbianism and homosexuality were integral to ancient Greek society and culture is overwhelmingly strong. Just as contemporary queer poets, historians, theorists, and activists are engaged in excavating the evidence of our continued existence, H.D. was similarly engaged, sifting through the fragments, reclaiming the adulterated stories, writing queers back into the record. And she did so with the awareness that such a revision does more than fill a gap, or simply supplement our knowledge, but that it radically reshapes the way we think. The reemergence of an awareness of queer participation in the creation of culture mars the smooth reflective surface of the myth of heterocentricity. Evidence of our existence and our subsequent erasure from the record becomes something that needs to be accounted for; clearly this erasure is the result of hundreds of years of attempts at heterocentric social and political engineering.

In ancient times, and more recently among cultures left untainted by the straight mind and the social formations it demands, the difference of queerness was often seen as a special gift, an identity that enabled extraordinary insight. In *Another Mother Tongue: Gay Words, Gay Worlds*,[6] Judy Grahn explains that in some cultures gay people have been revered "because we are able to identify with both sexes and can see into more than one world at once, having the capacity to see from more than one point of view at a time" (72). Such difference was acknowledged as useful and necessary to the well-being of the society at large, and was quite frequently afforded a social status that reflected this understanding.

Hence, in her search for the historical roots of contemporary gay and lesbian cultural practices and terminology, Judy Grahn found that

> there is a world-wide pattern, both in historical and modern times, of institutional Gay power, of special Gay functions within the context of societies. These include Gay spiritual magic, Gay shamanism, women warriors/sorcerers, healers, and diviners, and even pagan religious homosexualism with gods and spirits worshipped with homosexual sex. (104)

Much like Judy Grahn in *Another Mother Tongue*, H.D. found herself in a relationship that was radically altering her worldview, yet lost in a heterocentric society that has structured itself on the suppression and denial of queerness. As intelligent, well-read, and poetically inclined young women, each in her respective era, both Grahn and H.D. began to suspect that their own experiences were not simple aberrations from the social norm, but part of a submerged cultural tradition. Judy Grahn, as a mid-century lesbian coming out through the gay bar culture, began her search by tracing the origins of community symbols, such as the color lavender or the wearing of pinkie rings, and slang words such as *faggot* and *dyke*. H.D., having no "gay community" as we now know it, sought for the traces of her cultural heritage in the materials available to her at the time, and the mythologies and poetries of the ancient Greeks were the most obvious place to start.

The ancient stories offered a glimpse into a nonheterocentric culture, a culture that valued artistic, erotic, and mystical insight, where the performance of ritual was entwined with creativity, sexuality, and communication with the divine. Alongside and behind the often told stories of conquering male heroes and capricious male gods, H.D. discovered a world of powerful female figures, lesbian lyricists, homosexual lovers, and ambiguously gendered demigods. "Ancient History," she wrote in *Paint It Today*, "What had they taught her of the Delphian and the goddess of the Precipice? What had they told her of the stars and the brothers on their horses? What had they told her of Althea and the fountains in the market and the wild azaleas?" (86).

"Hermes of the Ways" was H.D.'s first published poem and the poem selected by Pound to launch the imagist movement. Pound and subsequent critics have referred to "Hermes of the Ways" as an effective demonstration of the new poetics. According to Pound, it adheres to all of the basic tenets of imagism: direct presentation of the subject in clear sparse language, no sentimental or flowery elaboration of emotion or symbol, and the use of free verse to develop a new rhythm, as opposed to more traditional dependence on metrical norms.

Later critics, while accepting Pound's initial assessment, have also noted that the poem already exceeds the strict definition of imagist techniques in that it depicts motion and conflict, enacted not in a single moment of recognition but over an extended period of time. According to Louis Martz in his introduction to the *Collected Poems*,[7] "Her poetry and her prose, like her own psyche, live at the seething junction of opposite forces" (xi), but "the doctrines of Imagism provided H.D. with a discipline that enabled her to control the surges that arose from the depths of her violently responsive nature" (xiii). As H.D.'s first publication, Martz sees "Hermes of the Ways" reflecting traits that have subsequently been seen to characterize H.D.'s particular style: her choice of an ancient mythological subject, the invocation of a god, the harsh outdoor setting, the clashing of forces between nature and culture, and the fascination with borderlines.

Even as these and other valid observations have been made about the poem, to my knowledge no critic has discussed the implications of H.D.'s particular choice of subject. Hermes is a bisexual trickster figure who has origins in the ancient matriarchal and tribal culture that preceded the patriarchal culture of the ancient Greeks.[8] In the modern world, he is best known as the herald and messenger of the gods for the ancient Greeks, and the god of roads, commerce, invention, cunning, and theft. In his identification with Mercury among the Romans, he is also the god of eloquence and science, and in his association by the Greeks with the Egyptian god Thoth, he is also known as the god of wisdom, magic, and learning, the inventor of letters and numbers, and the scribe of all the gods. Overall, he is a daemonic figure, the messenger who founds culture by stealing from the gods, the trickster figure with an unstable identity who can travel to and from various realms—hence his association with the crossroads.

In these classical incarnations, he is the god of four-way crossroads, and the Romans erected phallic-shaped stones called *herms* at such junctures. Eventually, this symbolism evolved into the cross adopted most prominently by Christianity, but also by other faiths. Carrying a caduceus, he could cross between the worlds of the living and the dead, an association with the cycles of death and rebirth eventually absorbed by the Christian figure of the resurrected Christ. In the Middle Ages the Neoplatonists gave him the name Hermes Trismegistus, Hermes the Thrice-Great-One, and described him not as a god but as a great ancient philosopher. He was said to be the founder of magic, astrology, alchemy, and other blends of science with mysticism. The word *hermetic* used to describe occult systems of knowledge derives from this association.

Since it is usually four-way crossroads that are considered sacred to Hermes, H.D.'s choice to invoke Hermes "of the triple pathways," alludes not only to Hermes Trismegistus, but also to Hecate Trevia—that is, "Hecate of the Three Ways," an incarnation of the Great Goddess of the pre-patriarchal systems of belief. The medieval characterization of Hermes Trismegistus as an historical figure associated with the number three (instead of four) hearkens back to his derivation from the most ancient of the gods, the threefold goddess. "From the earliest ages, the concept of the Great Goddess was a trinity," Walker tells us, "and the model for all subsequent trinities, female, male, or mixed" (1018). Hermes has his origins in the Triple Goddess as

one of the Aegean Great Mother's primal serpent-consorts, partaking of her wisdom because he was once a part of her. Like India's Ardhanarisvara—Kali and Shiva united in one body—Hermes was the original "hermaphrodite" united in one body with Aphrodite. Priests of Hermes wore artificial breasts and female garments to preside over Aphrodite's Cyprian temple in the guise of the god Hermaphrodite. (Walker, 395)

The transformations wrought upon the figure of Hermes over time delineates the encroachment of patriarchal thinking on the earlier matriarchal systems. Yet, traces of the old beliefs and practices bleed through the revisions, so that even in his most recent incarnation, as Hermes Trismegistus, he continues to represent daemonic powers and the blending of disparate forces. Robert Duncan claims that the Poetess's engagement with "a disturbing sex magic" is the source of her power and the reason for her cultural erasure. Certainly, this power is embodied by Hermes, and the reasons for his ongoing transformation are similarly based on the misogynist and homophobic responses necessary for the establishment of a heterosexist patriarchy. From the beginning of her career, H.D. understood that the absorption and appropriation of prior spiritual beliefs and cultural practices was one of Western patriarchy's most effective methods of gaining political and social control. At the same time, such methods, while effective, are not always thorough.

In "Hermes of the Ways," it is unclear precisely which version of Hermes H.D.'s speaker is addressing, but it is evident that she is choosing to invoke a mythical figure of ambiguous sexuality and occult knowledge to come to her aid. I would like to suggest that the indeterminacy of H.D.'s reference allows her to allude to Hermes' various incarnations simultaneously, and relates directly to her sense of the palimpsest. Over time, and in different contexts, the palimpsest came to mean many things for H.D., but its relation to the multiple identities of Hermes is a useful place to begin to explore its complexities. For the palimpsest contains multiple texts simultaneously. It is a spatial representation of "an intellectual and emotional complex in an instant of time." If the future of Western culture was to be written by the modernists, H.D. understood that it would not be done so on a clean slate.

In recovering the emergent traces of queer existence from the available cultural texts, H.D. was not willing to erase the more recent writing, for this writing was also part of our cultural inheritance. She understood that, taken together, the various layers of text formed a composite background against which her own consciousness and, by extension, modernist consciousness in general had formed. If she were to write queerness into the modernist future, it could only be done against the backdrop of cultural history.

Hermes of the Ways

The hard sand breaks,
and the grains of it
are clear as wine.

Far off over the leagues of it,
the wind,
playing on the wide shore,
piles little ridges,
and the great waves
break over it.

But more than the many-foamed ways

of the sea,
I know him
of the triple pathways,
Hermes,
who awaits.

Dubious,
facing three ways,
welcoming wayfarers,
he whom the sea-orchard
shelters from the west,
from the east
weathers sea-wind;
fronts the great dunes.

Wind rushes over the dunes,
and the coarse, salt-crusted grass
answers.

Heu,
it whips round my ankles!

II

Small is
this white stream,
flowing below ground
from the poplar-shaded hill,
but the water is sweet.

Apples on the small trees
are hard,
too small,
too late ripened
by a desperate sun
that struggles through sea-mist.

The boughs of the trees
are twisted
by many bafflings;
twisted are
the small-leafed boughs.

But the shadow of them
is not the shadow of the mast head
nor of the torn sails.

Hermes, Hermes,
the great sea foamed,
gnashed its teeth about me;
but you have waited,
where sea-grass tangles with
shore-grass.
                (*Collected Poems*, 37-39)

The masterful blending of modernist poetic techniques with ancient mythological subjects has often been seen as one of the most characteristic, yet disturbing, aspects of H.D.'s poetics. Yet, if we view the tensions created between content and form as H.D.'s expression of palimpsestic insight, we can see that the strange juxtapositions force a sense of continuity between the modernist present and our ancient origins, which could only be discovered by pulling back all of the layers of history. Implicit in the modernist cry to "Make it new!" was a desire for rebirth of the human spirit, a hope for regeneration of culture and renewal of beauty, and freedom from social and artistic conventions. Modernism was, by definition, forward-looking. But for H.D. in particular, the modernist search for spiritual renewal and visionary insight was ancient and universal as well. Hence, like Hermes in her poem, H.D. as *Imagiste*, Poetess, and queer visionary was looking three ways.

This palimpsestic depiction of Hermes is furthered by H.D.'s choice to set her invocation in a rough landscape rather than at an actual crossroads. Set amidst great dunes, the sea, and a sea-orchard, so few cultural markers are given that it is impossible to set the poem in historical time. The presence of the orchard and the mention of a mast head and torn sails (though the latter artifacts are mentioned for the purpose of negative comparison) indicate the existence of a civilization, but these products of culture are so basic and long-standing that they do not tie the setting to any particular period. Indeed, the sense of atemporality created in "Hermes of the Ways" and in many of the other poems from H.D.'s early volumes has been seen by some readers as evidence of her escapist tendencies. However, her speakers are often so vividly present, even in those poems that are clearly placed in ancient settings, that H.D. manages to convey a sense of contemporanaeity with their various situations. For example, in "Hermes of the Ways," although the speaker is addressing an ancient figure, all but the final stanza is written in the present tense, and in the last stanza of Part I, the speaker locates herself directly in the windy scene previously described, with the pained outcry "Heu,/it whips round my ankles!" Through this technique of creating a sense of contemporary involvement with a variety of distant pasts, H.D. was conveying an aspect of her visionary insight—the knowledge that time was not linear but fluid, that the past, present and the future were coexistent.

While the juxtaposition of cultural timelessness with the immediacy of the speaker's situation creates an ambiguity in the poem's temporal setting, "Hermes of the Ways" is equally ambiguous in spatial terms. Despite the studied precision of detail that is the trademark of imagist technique, it is impossible to locate either the speaker or Hermes with any certainty within the landscape presented. While the lines already quoted from the end of Part I seem to locate the speaker amidst the windy dunes, in the final stanza of Part II she implies that she had been shipwrecked and tossed on the shore. Since H.D. does not delineate any trek away from the shore and into the dunes, the question arises as to how and why she is located amidst the dunes at the end of Part I. The lines from the final stanza of Part II that imply her shipwreck, "the great sea foamed,/gnashed its teeth about me;/but you have waited," are the only lines in the poem not written in the present tense, so we could assume simply that time has elapsed, during which she changed her location. The rest of the final stanza implies that at the moment of the speaker's arrival on the shore Hermes is located in the dunes, "where sea-grass tangles with/shore-grass." Therefore we have a possible motive for her assumed trek into the dunes.

If we trace the poem from the beginning, it seems certain that in the first stanza, the speaker is immersed in the dunes where "The hard sand breaks," looking "Far off over the leagues of it," toward "the wide shore," and "the great waves" in Stanza 2. This stanza sets up a context wherein the speaker's visual scan of the scene moves increasingly into the distance so that, in the third stanza, when the first mention of Hermes (beyond the title) is made, it is implied that he is in the distance, at the shore. If the final stanza of the poem initially locates the speaker on the shore and Hermes in the dunes, and we assume she has made a journey toward him some time prior to the moment at which the poem opens, then his subsequent location at the shore when she is in the dunes would seem contradictory.

The third stanza and the last stanza are the only places within the poem where H.D.'s speaker names Hermes. In the first instance, she names him as "Hermes,/ who awaits." In the second instance, she directly addresses him: "Hermes. Hermes," and claims "but you have waited," an assertion which, through repetition, highlights what seems to be an aspect of his role or nature as a god. If Hermes is he "who awaits," then the paradox is that one can never fully meet him. He must always be located elsewhere, awaiting the speaker's arrival. Yet he is not absent from the scene, but fully present, awaiting; it is the speaker who has yet to arrive. This paradoxical nature of Hermes would therefore explain the shifting locations of the speaker and of Hermes: he can only be waiting where she is not.

The engagement with paradox is, of course, a central aspect of mystical thinking. By definition paradox defies reason: its literal meaning comes from the Greek, *paradoxes*, beyond what is thought. Epistemological systems based on rationality cannot engage this kind of thinking. It exceeds the bounds of logic; it escapes linearity and categorical definitions. Given H.D.'s personal inclinations toward mysticism and her attempts to write and think beyond the binary logic of the straight mind, it is hardly surprising, then, to find her engaging poetically with paradox from the start. In addition to playing a central role in the traditions of mysticism, paradox is a central aspect of the trickster figure as well. Paradox is the very essence of Hermes' identity: whether identified with the four-way crossroads, the triple nature of the Great Goddess, or the occult sciences of Trismegistus, he is its embodiment.

While the speaker seems to be caught in a paradoxical relation to Hermes in terms of her location in H.D.'s poem, Hermes' own placement in relation to the landscape described is even more problematic. In Stanza 4 we are given a litany of his qualities: "Dubious,/facing three ways,/ welcoming wayfarers," followed by a description of his location as he faces three ways. The first landmark seems stable enough: Hermes is "he whom the sea-orchard /shelters from the west." This is the first and only direct mention of the orchard and, as such, the key line for understanding the shift of locale in Part II. Perhaps because this location is a cultivated one, H.D. means to imply that it is more fixed than the shifting sands, grasses, winds, and seas, or perhaps she stabilizes its placement because the orchard is an image she is about to "cultivate" extensively within Part II.

A directional ambiguity begins to enter in the next pair of lines. Continuing with a seemingly parallel construction, H.D. repeats the structure and rhythm of "from the west" with "from the east," but the strength of the parallel is soon called into doubt with the subsequent line, "weathers sea-wind." The uncertainty arises in deciding where we imagine the wind blowing: directly from over the sea toward the shore, or from the shore toward the sea, or neither of these opposites, but crossways, along the length of shore, from either direction. This uncertainty of what lies to the east in turn undermines our previous certainty about the location of the orchard. In addition to this directional conundrum, the question arises as to how something located in the west can shelter one from an eastern wind. In any case, these four lines highlight the unreliability of dichotomous relations: while the oppositions involved seem to provide a certain degree of categorical stability, if one element shifts so must its complement. While we would expect H.D.'s use of oppositional terms such as east/west to clarify the scene, in fact these terms are so unstable in their interdependency within the poem as to be virtually meaningless.

It is also worth noting that in her use of directional terms, H.D. not only alludes to a system of binary oppositions, but also invokes the Roman version of Hermes as the god of four-way crossroads. Even as her language evokes this reference, however, it effaces it, since a four-directional system cannot represent H.D.'s Hermes "of the triple pathways." It is as if the poem itself is a palimpsest: while not fully erasing Hermes' association with the number four, H.D. is writing over that story in order to tell a "new" story of Hermes "facing three ways," and in doing so, breaches what should be a closed system of dichotomous relations and their multiples.

While the first two directional indicators of Hermes' locale slide into indeterminacy in their relation to each other, the third direction Hermes faces slides into another kind of ambiguity. In its brevity, the line "fronts the great dunes" is seemingly unambiguous. The line conveys a further sense of clarity and closure with its end-stopped construction and its placement as the final line of the stanza. Yet, H.D.'s use of the word "fronts" is duplicitous. It can mean that Hermes *faces* the great dunes or that he is looking in the opposite direction as he stands *in front of* the great dunes. In the context provided by the poem, either interpretation can apply.

Hence, throughout Stanza 4, in which H.D. is ostensibly fixing Hermes' location for us, we cannot ascertain with any clarity Hermes' position in relation either to the landmarks she provides, or to the speaker present at the scene. We cannot firmly imagine even the placement of the elements of the threefold landscape—seashore, dunes, and sea-orchard—in relation to one another within the topography indicated. In her use of binary relations and quaternary directional systems, H.D. belies the stability of those systems. By introducing paradoxical relations and duplicitous meanings, she is invoking the elements such systems are meant to exclude. The poem itself is "grounded" in a paradox: even as H.D. indicates the inadequacies of such systems for describing her apprehension of a triple god, she does manage to invoke, at least fragmentarily, Hermes of the triple pathways, in his aspect as the god of paradox, duplicity, and ambiguity, the god of in-between states.

Throughout *Sea Garden*, several of H.D.'s poems utilize flower imagery to highlight what Louis Martz has called "the basic theme of the entire volume: the `beauty' that results from the fierce clashing of natural forces" (*Collected Poems*, xi). He cites poems such as "Sea Rose," "Sea Poppies," and "Sheltered Garden," among others, as "only the most obvious examples" of H.D.'s preference for the toughened product of these clashing forces over the soft sweetness of the more cultivated blooms. In "Sea Rose," for example, H.D. writes:

> Rose, harsh rose,
> marred and with stint of petals,
> meager flower, thin,
> sparse of leaf,
>
> more precious
> than a wet rose
> single on a stem—
> (*Collected Poems*, 5)

And in "Sheltered Garden," her aversion to cultivated "beauty" is so strong it fills her with a longing for its violent destruction:

> For this beauty,
> beauty without strength,
> chokes out life.
> I want wind to break,
> scatter these pink-stalks,
> snap off their spiced heads,
> fling them about with dead leaves—
> (*Collected Poems*, 20)

However, H.D.'s disdain for conventional botanical aesthetics is more than an angry rejection of the norm; it also contains a longing for another aesthetic standard, "a new beauty" she has yet to find:

> O to blot out this garden
> to forget, to find a new beauty
> in some terrible
> wind-tortured place.
> (*Collected Poems*, 21)

In Part II of "Hermes of the Ways," H.D. provides us with a more fully developed image of such a place: the sea-orchard. Here, she expands the beauty she finds in a single tortured sea rose into an entire grove, but the elements of scarring and distorted growth, resulting from the struggle for life amidst inhospitable conditions, are still present. As with "Sea Rose," where H.D. works against conventional connotation in her use of the adjectives "harsh" and "meager," the various elements of the sea orchard are described as "small," "hard," and "twisted." Although H.D.'s preference for this "new beauty" is not stated as directly in "Hermes of the Ways" as it is in poems such as "Sea Rose," and "Sheltered Garden," it is still clearly indicated.

After the tumult of wind, sand, and water of Part I, the sea-orchard seems serene, despite its meager offerings. The preponderance of *s*, *w*, *h*, and *r* sounds works to soften the tone, as well as the gentle connotations of H.D.'s word choices, for example, *stream, flowing, sweet, sea-mist, boughs, shadow*. In addition, her verb usage shifts drastically between the first and second parts, furthering the image of the orchard as a refuge from the continual motion of the previous scene. As in Part I, the first four stanzas of Part II are set in the present, but in Part II, the main verb in each stanza is the verb "to be." The active verbs of Part I have receded into modifying and adjectival phrase. The implication is that the sea-orchard exists as a model of survival; it is a state of being, which, though hard and small, seems to offer the speaker a reprieve from her previous struggles.

Eschewing the linearity of a chronological telling, H.D. withholds until the last two stanzas the original reason for the speaker's arrival at this rough place: that she has survived a shipwreck. This belated allusion to the violent motion of the sea further indicates why she has sought refuge at the difficult and unstable "crossroads" where Hermes awaits. The place (or places) where he waits, however harsh and unstable, is less violent and dangerous than where she's been. Referring to the twisted boughs of the sea-orchard trees, H.D. writes:

> But the shadow of them
> is not the shadow of the mast head
> nor of the torn sails.

With its brevity and direct syntactical construction, the stanza has the tone of an assertion, indicating that the speaker is decisive in her preference for the "new beauty" of this orchard. At the same time, the language of the image she constructs here is rife with indirection. H.D. uses a subdued simile to draw a comparison between the speaker's previous experience and the sea-orchard. True to the imagists' desire to make the language direct and concrete, H.D. omits the comparative words "like" or "as," but the association between the "twisted...small-leafed boughs" and "the mast head" and "torn sails" is fully established. Yet, her simile functions through contrast: she evokes a comparison only to negate its applicability. What is highlighted through this image, then, is the dissimilarity between the remnants of her previous "place" (the ship that brought her here) and her current locale.

In a further move of indirection, H.D. contrasts not the things themselves, but their shadows, and the import of these shadows can be interpreted in several ways. In a platonic worldview, the shadow of the thing itself represents a dilution of the "real," a vision better suited to our meager human comprehension; or a shadow indicates an expansion of the thing beyond itself, a range of influence. In its blockage of light, a shadow offers either the sinister connotation of a looming threat, or it can be read as a welcome refuge from a broiling sun.

The final stanza of Part II (and therefore of the poem) continues the allusion to a shipwreck begun in the penultimate stanza, but it is structurally unlike any of the preceding stanzas. It is the only stanza in which the speaker addresses Hermes directly. As such, it functions as an invocation, although it is more usual to place an apostrophic stanza toward the beginning of the poem. Furthermore, it is the only stanza written in the past tense, and hence the only stanza to refer directly to events beyond the immediate setting H.D. has created throughout the rest of the poem. In speaking directly to Hermes and referring to events beyond the scope of the poem, H.D. is implying that a personal relationship exists between the speaker and Hermes.

Indeed, the speaker's sense of intimate connection with the god of the crossroads seems to be the central theme of the entire poem; the imagistic presentation of sand, sea, and orchard serves as a vehicle for conveying her apprehension of his triple-faced nature. And here we must confront one of the paradoxes of H.D.'s situation as a visionary poet utilizing the techniques of imagism. The imagist principles that call for direct presentation of the thing, whether subjective or objective, cannot be applied to a god, a daemonic presence. We cannot gaze upon him directly, unless we ourselves quest for him in our own visions. H.D. knew that the visionary could not cause us to behold her vision. Hence, she could only present her apprehension of Hermes of the Ways indirectly, by creating a fictional persona, the shipwrecked speaker, and then by focusing our attention not on the speaker's vision of Hermes, but on the places he has drawn the speaker to, the surroundings that fall within his gaze.

This sense of personal connection to ancient gods and other figures from mythology and H.D.'s attraction to the territories they inhabit have frequently provoked critics to seek biographical connections with her poetry. At the same time, H.D.'s critics have often assumed that her use of indirection and her tendency to create dramatic personae is an attempt at evasion, the implication being that she is hiding behind a mask out of shyness, shame, or fear. However, if we revise our image of the Poetess from the meek, overly sensitive "lady poet" to an image of the self-empowering shaman-poet seeking her history and attempting to convey her apprehension of nonheterocentric consciousness, H.D.'s use of personae, indirection, ambiguity, and paradox can be seen as deliberately chosen techniques for conveying her insights with as much clarity as possible. Motivated by the need to open up social/intellectual/psychic space for queer existence, H.D. sought, in the freedom of modernism, to piece together the significance of her personal experiences through the techniques of imagism within the palimpsest of myth. This is the ancient role of the Poetess, the role

H.D. recreated for herself. In *Another Mother Tongue*, Judy Grahn has described this office:

In tribal culture we often formed a pool of potential initiates some of whom became the shamans and medicine people who can enter the spirit world, the wind, the mountains and rivers and the bottom of the sea; the worlds of the dead, or spirits, of other people's minds, of the gods and their forces; we it is who bring back the strange and old messages, interpreting them for the benefit of our tribe. Anciently we were sometimes rewarded and esteemed for this. (Grahn, 273)

The difficulty in reading H.D.'s poetry arises not because she was being intentionally obscurantist in regard to the facts of her life, but because she was attempting to convey "another state of emotional life or being, a life of being that contained the past and the future." When read for biographical correlations, her poetry seems obscure because she was writing philosophically, as a mystic, and not autobiographically. This is not to say that H.D. excluded the facts of her sexual life and her emotional responses from her poetry; to the contrary, these experiences comprised the basis of her insight. Yet, the experiences themselves were not her primary subjects. Instead, H.D. focussed on the "emotional and intellectual complex in an instant of time" described by Pound as the essence of imagism, which is also the essence of visionary apprehension. In her poetry, H.D. utilized myth as a vehicle for expressing her experience and insight in a "common language," even though she had to select and reanimate the images of mythology with a "new" consciousness in order to affirm the commonality of her own existence. It is in her prose works, not her poetry, that she presents the biographical events informing her poetics.

Yet, even in her prose writing, H.D. strove to convey much more than the facts of her life; she wanted to convey the inner experience of the events and people she involved herself in. In this, she is similar to other early modernists, as Robert Duncan asserts in *The H.D. Book*: "these writers of the new interior monologue read their lives as the Kabbalists read the Torah, exploring the permutation of meaning in each letter and diacritical mark...the ordeal of the contemporary psyche was to create the meaning of its life" (72).

Throughout her career, H.D. experimented with various styles and approaches in her prose writing in an attempt to capture consciousness as it interacts with the world, as the mind responds to its environment in the present moment. In her tendency toward abstraction, repetition, and obsession, in her use of stream of consciousness, with her strange juxtapositions and wild associational leaps, H.D.'s prose style is not unlike Gertrude Stein's ongoing literary exploration of her own theory of the continuous present. In *Her*, for example, H.D.'s exposition is devoted primarily to her depiction of this inner life. She doesn't use it for establishing setting or for developing plot. "Plot" emerges only through dialogue—people's reactions to the H.D. figure, Hermione, their opinions, words, are the "plot." The physical environment is presented obsessively, but only through Her's eyes; the reader receives "reality" filtered only through Her's consciousness, but told to us by an omniscient third-person narrator. Through this narrative strategy H.D. creates a layered text, oddly unstable in the shifting perspectives on Her's own self-consciousness. In recounting her past, H.D. interpolates her current awareness into the situation, while simultaneously confining the narrative only to the immediate events and ideas occurring within Hermione's immediate locale. The effect is one of intimacy and estrangement, reflecting once again her interest in the temporal aspects of the palimpsest, this time in relation to the terrain of the inner self:

She could not know that the reason for failure of a somewhat exaggeratedly-planned "education," was possibly due to subterranean causes. She had not then dipped dust-draggled, intellectual plumes into the more modern science that posts signs over emotional bog and intellectual lagoon ("failure complex," "compensation reflex") to show us where we may or where we may not stand. Carl Gart, her father, had been wont to shrug away psychology as a "science." Hermione Gart could not then know that her precise reflection, her entire failure to conform to expectations was perhaps some subtle form of courage.

It was summer. She wasn't now any good for anything. Her Gart looked up into liriodendron branches and flat tree leaf became, to her, lily pad on green pool. She was drowned now. She could no longer struggle. Clutching out toward some definition of herself, she found that "I am Her Gart" didn't let her hold on. Her fingers slipped off; she was no longer anything. Gart, Gart, Gart and the Gart theorem of mathematical biological intention dropped out Hermione. She was not Gart, she was not Hermione, she was not anymore Her Gart, what was she? (Her, 4)

"The definition of self, the penetration into self, was H.D.'s preoccupation and obsession," writes Barbara Guest (xii). Paradoxically, what emerges from H.D.'s obsessive self-consciousness is not a solipsistic self-centeredness, but a heightened social awareness. The story she told again and again is the story of what H.D. considered to be one of the most formative periods of her life: her young adulthood, the period in which her sexual and social identity was most in flux. In her autobiographical novels, H.D. depicts herself as she struggled to create an autonomous self-definition; and through this self-exploration H.D. attained a heightened awareness of the range of social forces that raged against her attainment of sexual and social autonomy.

For H.D., as with most queer youth, even today, her first encounter with the limitations of the straight mind took place within her family of origin, and by extension, the white middle-class culture of turn-of-the-century mainstream America to which her family belonged. Reflecting on this initial resistance to her emerging queerness in *Paint It Today*, H.D. was perhaps insulted but not necessarily surprised:

It was natural that she and Josepha and such as she and Josepha should be cast out of the mass of the living, out of the living body, as useless as natural wastage, excrementitious, it is true, thrown out of the mass, projected forth, crystallized out, orient pearls, to stand forever after, a reflection somehow, on the original rasped and wounded parent. (*Paint It Today*, 18)

From the normative vantage point of the straight mind, H.D. understood that lesbianism was so anomalous to its way of thinking that it could only be rejected and abhorred. To a heterocentric culture, she was "useless as natural wastage," literally, *worth shit*, "excrementitious." Yet, because she is an outcast from the "natural" order of heterocentricity, she does not share its values. Hence, in her own estimation, lesbians "such as she and Josepha" are "orient pearls." Years later, in *The Walls Do Not Fall* (1944), H.D. would describe the visionary knowledge she had gained through her ongoing explorations of the palimpsest of sexual identity as "that pearl-of-great-price" (*Collected Poems*, 514). Even as her queerness necessarily estranged her from both her particular parents and from the dominant culture, H.D. understood that this estrangement was necessary for the maintenance and creation of a heterocentric culture. As outcast other, she was nevertheless a product of that "living body" of family and community, and as such, her role was to allow the culture to identify itself against the "difference" of her sexuality. In undergoing the ostracizing effects of homophobia, H.D. understood that the parent culture, its myths and psychology, relied on her queer existence to serve as "a reflection somehow," on the master narrative of heterocentrism, to aid in its self-creation through contrast.

What H.D. did not immediately understand, however, was how broadly heterosexism is woven throughout the consciousness of modern Western culture. She simply assumed that this narrow-mindedness was a "natural" result of the parochialism of the American middle class. In Europe, among the other outcasts, the *cognoscenti*, H.D. expected things to be different for "she and Josepha." For H.D., the awakening of a modernist consciousness necessarily involved a critical stance toward heterosexist social structures and heterocentric worldviews. She soon discovered that the relevance of this particular critique was not as apparent to everyone involved in the various attempts to "Make it new!":

But it came as a shock to find they were separated not only from the masses but also from the refined, the sensuous, the artistically differentiated as well.... Somehow, they had imagined, speaking the same language, bred in the same tradition, that in London they would find their own. It was not so.

Language and tradition do not make a people, but the heat that presses on them, the cold that baffles them, the alternating lengths of night and day. (*Paint It Today*, 20)

"Her ecstatic response to the forces of nature is characteristic: it is the union of self with nature that she creates in her famous 'Oread' (1914)," writes Louis Martz. "To live constantly at the juncture of such forces, inner and outer, to inhabit constantly the borderline—this was to be the life that lay ahead for H.D., as person and as poet" (*Collected Poems*, xiv). In understanding the extent to which H.D. was fully aware of how the pressures of heterosexism and the alienating effects of homophobia were at work in her life, we can begin to comprehend the relevance of her preoccupation with depicting "such forces, inner and outer" within the "escapist" landscapes and ancient "masks" in her poems. Within her imagistic explorations of orchard boughs "twisted /by many bafflings;" and the "heat /that presses up and blunts /the points of pears /and rounds the grapes" ("Garden"), H.D. is working directly with the material of her life.

Masquerade and evasion was never the impetus behind H.D.'s poetics; rather, she was inspired, as many mystics are, by "The drive /to connect. The dream of a common language"[9]—in defiance of the ostracization she suffered. The pressure to repress any "deviance," the fear of discovery such closeting produces, and the alienation that results from capitulating to the heterosexist social norm would be an act of masking and evasion, and H.D. never did fully capitulate to the demands of that worldview. Even in her heterosexual involvements, she maintained her sense of bisexual identity, choosing men like the young Ezra Pound and Richard Aldington, each of whom, at the time, seemed to comprehend the necessity of breaking away from the rigid social/sexual traditions in order to "Make it new!" Eventually, each of these men proved themselves to be more traditional in their sexual politics than disruptive, and H.D. came to see this and knew she had to let them go. Accepting as valid their indoctrination by the straight mind, or perhaps not even seeing it as indoctrination, seeing heterosexism as *natural*, neither Pound nor Aldington could fully share in her queer shamanistic vision. Reflecting on the changes from the earliest flush of enthusiastic excitement of modernist thinking to an eerie conservatism brought on by the "dark wall" (65) of World War I, in *Paint It Today*, H.D. observed that "certain prejudices and protective customs were curiously strengthened; almost Victorian prejudices and conventions sprang to life among the apparently advanced of the prewar period" (68).

The isolation she was made to feel in her sexual "deviance" (first, at home in Pennsylvania, then among the artists and writers in London, and again, among her friends and associates during and after the war) was something she could attempt to undo. "Divination is working with things to release the content and form of a future or fate," writes Robert Duncan in the *H.D. Book* (38). As H.D. searched through the emotions, insights, and memories of her personal history for meaning, she drew parallels with ancient stories; in doing so, she became less isolated. It connected her to humanity, even as her society and culture worked to make her feel "excrementitious."

In *Love and the Western World*, a book H.D. sometimes referred to as her "textbook," Denis de Rougemont wrote "that the erotic and the mystical speak the same language" (Guest, 329). Throughout her life, H.D.'s erotic attachments were the source of her mysticism, the catalyst for mystical experiences. Dredging through the remnants of ancient mysteries as they are embodied in myth, H.D. found emotional and psychological correlations to her personal life. Hence, in her poetic explorations of mythic material, H.D. was not only seeking images of queerness, role models if you will, and new ways of thinking (or the recovery of ancient, pre-heterocentric ways); she was also seeking to establish a personal connection to the "truths" of the tales. Emotionally, sexually, and psychically, the gods and settings of the ancient myths were true for H.D. The mythologies were chosen because of their relevance to her circumstances; they helped her clarify herself.

Beginning with her earliest "imagist" poems and continuing throughout her subsequent poetic development, H.D.'s fascination with the poetics of shamanism grew. With increasing frequency she turned her pen toward the chant, the incantation, the apostrophe, the direct address, the dramatic monologue, the reply, the chorus, the rite; all of these are extensions of oral and sacred traditions. As Robert Duncan remarked, H.D. developed an understanding that "there is not one myth alone but a gathering of myths. Here the poet does not see the language as a system but as a community of meanings as deep and wide as the nature of man has been" (47).

Throughout her youth, H.D. sought others like herself, sacred lesbian prophets "such as she and Josepha." Initially, in her relationship with Frances Gregg, and later, from 1918 until the end of her life in 1961 in her relationship with Bryher, she did find others like herself. In her poetic explorations of the palimpsest of myth, H.D. found confirmation of their connections to world history, as diviners of the sacred, travelers into the liminal spaces, dwellers of the borderline. In *Another Mother Tongue* Judy Grahn writes:

Homosexuals, and others who serve similar social functions, such as circus people, artists and musicians, prostitutes and clowns, are not living on the "fringe." This is an inaccurate image. The universe, let us say instead, consists of interlocking worlds. Gay culture is always on the cusp of each interlocking world or way of life, on the path between one world and another. This is why Hekate and Afrikete were worshipped at the crossroads. (270)

In seeking an expression of her palimpsestic insights through poetry, H.D. sought to cultivate a queer poetics in which the fragmentation by heterosexist patriarchy of sexual passion, mystical vision, and poetic ecstasy would be repaired. Hers was a healing vision. As the nature of visionary insight is fragmentary, and merely glimpsed, imagism provided a strong starting point for the development of her own poetic technique, of broadening the scope of her personal insights into a vision of a historical palimpsest.

In reading myths as the palimpsest of civilization, H.D. found the same elements constantly reconfigured: sexuality, song, spiritual questing; Eros, the sacred, the poetic incantation; the exploration of consciousness and sexual identity, visionary encounters with the holy, and the creative expression of that encounter. Reading the myths as layered texts, H.D. strove to crystallize the emotional "truth" of a mythologized moment. Doing this made her own experiences more broadly significant; they became transpersonal. The explorations of her own psyche reacting to these clashing forces could be read, through myth, as a personal engagement with the writing of human history, as though her psyche were in a palimpsestic relation to the primal settings and the ancient myths: "For every life contains the world and sometimes the world is not big enough to contain one life" (*Paint It Today*, 27).

NOTES

1. Throughout this chapter, I have relied on Barbara Guest, *Herself Defined: The Poet H.D. and Her World* (New York: Doubleday, 1984 for historical and biographical data. The first annual anthology, *Des Imagistes* (1914), was published under the editorial control of Pound, even though he had already moved on to vorticism. The change in name indicates the shift of editorial control from Pound to Lowell (Guest, 56-71).

2. For example, *Bid Me To Live (A Madrigal)*, (New York Dial Press, 1960) and *End to Torment: A Memoir of Ezra Pound* (New York: New Directions, 1979).

3. *HERmione* (New York: New Directions, 1981), *Asphodel* (Durham, N. C.: Duke University Press, 1992), *Paint It Today* (New York: New York University Press, 1992). Throughout this chapter, I will refer to *HERmione* by H.D.'s title *Her*.

4. Robert Duncan, "The H.D. Book Part Two: Nights and Days Chapter 9," *Chicago Review* 30, no.3 (1979): 40.

5. Eileen Gregory, "Rose Cut in Rock: Sappho and H.D.'s *Sea Garden*," *Contemporary Literature* 27, no.4 (Winter 1986): 525.

6. Judy Grahn, *Another Mother Tongue: Gay Words, Gay Worlds* (Boston: Beacon Press, 1984).

7. H. D., *Collected Poems: 1912-1944*, Louis L. Martz, ed. (New York: New Directions, 1983), xi. In addition to Martz's introduction, all poetry by H.D. cited in this chapter is from this edition.

8. The following entries in Barbara Walker, *The Women's Encyclopedia of Myths and Secrets* (San Francisco: Harper and Row, 1983) were useful in writing this section: "Crossroads" (190-191); "Hecate" (378-379), "Hermes" (395-398), and "Trinity" (1018-1020).

9. Adrienne Rich, *The Dream of a Common Language: Poems 1974-1977*, (New York: W. W. Norton, 1978), 7.

Afterword

It was almost two o'clock in the morning, and I was up, writing about H.D. This city is small, it mostly goes to sleep at night. Sometimes I think I hear the slow and deep breathing of sleepers, the inward whistle, the outward sigh of each one tumbling out the windows of the city, caught on an updraft, gathered into a collective rhythm, and carried to me through my open window on the chill early morning breeze. Occasionally, a car passes beneath my window, a siren sings in the distance, a group of friends walk home from a party, around the corner, someone is finally getting dropped off from work. These things happen quietly, one by one; unlike the hectic simultaneity of the daytime hours, the night is long and nearly empty. Those of us who are still awake know a different pace. When the city is asleep, I can think.

This night I was thinking about H.D., about how she knew she had to leave America to be free, or at least to make the attempt at freedom. I was thinking about how, once away from her family, from Philadelphia, and perhaps from the exigencies of white middle-class womanhood, she was caught by surprise at the homophobia among the people she sought as artistic comrades, as friends. In arriving at what she hoped would be a refuge from the pressures of heterosexist social values, H.D. soon found that even in expatriation, there would be no true escape. Just then, as I was thinking of this, a car roared loudly from up the street. As it passed my house, a hate-filled scream of "Faggots!" tore through the night.

Most likely, it was not directed personally at me. It was merely a coincidence that the car was directly below my window when the enraged male screamer let loose his assault. He could have been yelling at someone walking down the street, or at any one of a dozen queer households on this block, or at random because he knew that this is the neighborhood where many gay people live.

The relative calm of after midnight is always tentative. Night in the city, any city of any size, has never really been safe, though there are long moments when

I can feel unharassed, free. I suppose H.D. decided that an endangered freedom was better than not knowing freedom at all. She chose to remain expatriated for nearly fifty years.

H.D., of course, was not the only queer modernist to expatriate from her native land. Gertrude Stein and Alice Toklas never returned to live in America, though both of them had great affection and pride in their native country and its people. It took nearly forty years and two world wars for the American public (including many literati) to reciprocate any of this affection and pride. Mina Loy expatriated from her native England at her earliest opportunity, variously living in France, Italy, the United States, and Mexico. She eventually settled permanently in the United States, where she began to be "forgotten." Djuna Barnes returned from her expatriation, but soon began her withdrawal from her modernist friends and associates, which led to a nearly complete seclusion lasting almost forty years. The mystique around her reclusiveness would be of the same mythic proportions as that surrounding Emily Dickinson, if her standing in the literary canon were more stable Amy Lowell was not a recluse, but like Dickinson, remained in her family home. She did not need to expatriate, because she had the inheritance of class privilege to protect her and Ada Dwyer against the financial deprivations an economic system structured on heterosexism can impose on queers. Yet, her economic advantage did not lessen her sense of cultural defiance as a lesbian modernist poet; nor did it protect her from homophobic reactions and jeers directed both at her aesthetic experiments and her physical person.

The depth of violent loathing I heard in that young man's voice was startling, frightening. Why does he hate queers so deeply, so viscerally that he is compelled to scream into the night? I'm sure he had no knowledge of the irony of the situation as he juxtaposed his shouted epithet against my writing on the cultural presence of queers. Alongside the automatic terror he intended to provoke, I held a feeling of distressed amazement at the breach between his worldview and mine.

To many critics and scholars over the years, and certainly to the millions of late-twentieth-century Americans who don't read poetry at all, it matters very little that Ezra Pound made dismissive jokes about "Amygism" or wrote cruel verses about Djuna Barnes as being "none too cuddly." Of course, a single epithet hurled from a speeding car in itself is perhaps not too harmful; it's the history of burning queers the term evokes that is frightening, it is the threat of future repetitions wherein lies the danger. It is the palimpsestic aspects of terms such as "faggot" and its cognates that we cannot afford to ignore. Our lives may depend on it; one can never be sure of whether or when the tide of scapegoating and persecution will rise and turn against us once again. Ezra Pound felt it necessary to remind Hilda Doolittle and Frances Gregg that "you and she should have been burnt as witches" (*Her*, 172). Why did he need to say that, and, according to H.D., on more than one occasion?

It is often said that one hates what one fears, and I do not underestimate the magnitude of the "threat" the acknowledgment of queer existences poses to the social order. Incidents such as witch burnings and gay bashings, the internment of queers in Nazi death-camps, or the incarceration of contemporary gay teens in psychiatric hospitals where their "gender dysphoria" can be "corrected" by electroshock treatments may comprise the more extreme reactions to our existence, but such violent antigay and lesbian persecution has occurred continually throughout Western history. The eradication of our cultural visibility and viability is a necessary component of the maintenance of a heterocentric regime, and the use of actual violence or the ongoing threat of homophobic violence has been a traditional tool for assuring our compliance with the laws of erasure.

Nor do I underestimate the degree of anxiety the challenge we pose arouses on the personal as well as the social and political levels. Lesbian, gay, bisexual, queer, or nonheterocentric people, in going against the assumptions of a heterocentric worldview, are challenging some of the most precious core beliefs on which much of Western culture has relied. This is why, more often than not, our refusal to comply with heterosexist demands for silence and invisibility provokes such emotionally charged strong reactions and violent backlashes.

Not long ago I saw this in the local paper:[1] "Utah's Legislature voted Thursday to ban gay student clubs in high schools." Republican Representative David Bresnahan backed the measure:

"Statements were made that (youngsters) aren't recruited, and they sure are," he said, his voice breaking with emotion.

"Free speech does not include recruiting them into a homosexual lifestyle that can kill them."

Sen. George Mantes, a Democrat, called it "another moral witch-hunt in our state."

Although gay men and lesbians have been participants in the theorizing of sexual desires and identities from the moment such discussions began, the straight mind still exerts the greatest influence over the public discourse on queer existence. Even as we have increased the visibility of our participation in such discourses over time, so that today, we can overtly refer to the more academic of our discursive practices as "queer theory," the political forces of the straight mind have been astonishingly persistent as well as creative in their attempts to articulate the exact nature of the threat they feel from us. Variously throughout Western history and simultaneously within today's discourses, we have been deemed agents of Satan, sexual predators, biological freaks, mentally ill, national security risks, public health threats, amoral, simply mistaken, or nonexistent.

I do not know which of these heterocentric theories the hostile young man in the passing car subscribes to, and it hardly matters, for any and all of these claims are merely the mythologies of a social order, the "truths" that serve to justify the dominance of a certain epistemological system, that of the straight mind. In the worldview shared by all the hostile men (and occasionally, women) who like to shout venomously from speeding vehicles or speak out from their emotional distress to legislative bodies across America, my existence "is simply an impossibility," as Monique Wittig has said. A full acceptance of queer existence would destroy much of the world as we now know it,

since to do this would mean to reject the possibility of the constitution of the other and to reject the "symbolic order," to make the constitution of meaning impossible, without which no one can maintain an internal coherence. Thus lesbianism, homosexuality, and the societies that we form cannot be thought of or spoken of, even though they have always existed. (Wittig, 1992:28)

During the same month queer support groups were being outlawed in Utah, the new governor of New York State extended the previous governor 's executive order "barring state agencies from discrimination based on sexual orientation." There was, of course, opposition from those who think that New York, like Utah, should be more proactive in its fight against queer existence. Michael Long, state Conservative party chairman, voiced his objection to "giving credence to an alternate lifestyle that is abnormal and, quite frankly, doesn't give Western Civilization any pluses."[2]

Of the numerous slogans that have emerged from the contemporary struggle for queer visibility, there are two I especially enjoy: "We are everywhere," and "We're here. We're queer. Get used to it." Throughout this study, I've tried to indicate the variety of strategies each poet developed for living and writing both within and beyond the structures of heterosexist social organization and thinking. I do not believe there is a single way to formulate resistance to oppression; nor is oppression single issued or monolithic in its forms.

The oppressive paradigm of dichotomizing oppositions, which I have here called heterocentric thought, pervades our understandings of history, language, and social institutions. It has been the basic assumption underlying Western culture's constructions of individual identity, of sexuality, of consciousness. As ingenious as the defense of the dominant discourse may be in deflecting our focus, the fact is that the real struggle is between fundamentally different epistemologies.

Only a few of the possible methods for making our "impossibility" comprehensible have been explored here: in the palimpsest of history H.D. explored, the history of language Barnes reclaimed, the structures of heterosexist institutions Loy deconstructed, the grammatical structures of patriarchal language Stein exploded, the strength and beauty of the erotic Lowell asserted, and the forces of meter and categorical certainty Dickinson quietly undermined. There are a multiplicity of other possibilities not yet named, perhaps not yet even created. Queers can be even more ingenious than homophobes. Despite a formidable array of constraints and impediments,

Gay poets and writers continue the ancient functions of guiding, disturbing, recreating human thought and cultural values....And using the ancient chaotic powers, Gay trickster queens of all descriptions keep the matrix of human thought in the disrupted, tumultuous state that prevents stagnation and keeps true creativity and flexibility possible. (Grahn, 1984:231)

NOTES

1. *Times Union*, Albany, N.Y., Friday, April 19, 1996, A-7.
2. Ibid., Albany, N.Y., Wednesday, April 10, 1996, A-7.

Works Cited and Consulted

Abel, Elizabeth. *Writing and Sexual Difference*. Chicago: University of Chicago Press, 1982.

Barnes, Djuna. *The Book of Repulsive Women: 8 Rhythms and 5 Drawings*. The Outcast Chapbooks, no. 14. Yonkers, N.Y.: Alicat Bookshop Press, 1948.

———. *Nightwood*. New York: New Directions, 1961.

———. *Ladies Almanack*. Elmwood Park, Ill.: Dalkey Archive Press, 1992.

Barthes, Roland. *The Pleasure of the Text*. New York: Hill and Wang, 1973.

Bennett, Paula. *My Life a Loaded Gun: Dickinson, Plath, Rich and Female Creativity*. Boston: Beacon Press, 1986.

Benstock, Shari. *Women of the Left Bank*. Austin: University of Texas Press, 1986.

Bloom, Harold. *The Anxiety of Influence*. New York: Oxford University Press, 1973.

———, ed. *H.D.* New York: Chelsea House Publishers, 1989.

Bridgman, Richard. *Gertude Stein in Pieces*. New York: Oxford University Press, 1970.

Broe, Mary Lynn, ed. *Silence and Power: A Reevaluation of Djuna Barnes*. Carbondale: Southern Illinois University Press, 1991.

Buck, Claire. *H.D. and Freud: Bisexuality and a Feminine Discourse*. New York: St. Martin's Press, 1991.

Bulkin, Elly, and Joan Larkin, eds. *Lesbian Poetry: An Anthology*. Watertown, Mass.: Persephone Press, 1981.

Burke, Carolyn. *Becoming Modern:The Life of Mina Loy*. New York, N. Y.: Farrar, Straus and Giroux, 1996.

Burnett, Gary. *H.D. Between Image and Epic: The Mysteries of Her Poetics*. Ann Arbor: UMI Research Press, 1990.

Butler, Judith. *Gender Trouble: Feminism and the Subversion of Identity*. New York: Routledge, 1990.

Castle, Terry. *The Apparitional Lesbian: Female Homosexuality and Modern Culture*. New York: Columbia University Press, 1993.

Cixous, Helene, and Catherine Clement. *The Newly Born Woman*. Minneapolis: University of Minnesota Press, 1986.

Cruikshank, Margaret, ed. *Lesbian Studies: Present and Future*. Old Westbury, N.Y.: Feminist Press, 1982.

Culler, Jonathan. *On Deconstruction: Theory and Criticism After Structuralism*. Ithaca, N.Y.: Cornell University Press, 1982.

Daly, Mary. *Gyn/Ecology: The Metaethics of Radical Feminism*. Boston: Beacon Press, 1978.

DeKoven, Marianne. *A Different Language: Gertrude Stein's Experimental Writing*. Madison: University of Wisconsin Press, 1983.

De Lauretis, Teresa, ed. *Feminist Studies/Critical Studies*. Bloomington: Indiana University Press, 1986.

Dickinson, Emily. *The Complete Poems of Emily Dickinson*. Ed. T. H. Johnson. Boston: Little, Brown, 1960.

Donovan, Josephine. *Feminist Literary Criticism: Explorations in Theory*. Lexington: University Press of Kentucky, 1975.

Duncan, Robert. "The H.D. Book Part Two: Nights and Days Chapter 9." *Chicago Review* 30, no. 3 (1979): 37-88.

DuPlessis, Rachel Blau. "Romantic Thralldom in H.D." *Contemporary Literature* 20, no.2 (Summer 1979): 78-82.

———."For the Etruscans." In *The New Feminist Criticism*, Ed. Elaine Showalter. New York: Pantheon Books, 1985.

———.*The Pink Guitar: Writing as Feminist Practice*. New York: Routledge, 1990.

Eagleton, Terry. *Literary Theory: An Introduction*. Minneapolis: University of Minnesota Press, 1983.

Eisenstein, Hester, and Alice Jardine, eds. *The Future of Difference*. Boston: Hall, 1980.

Faderman, Lillian. *Odd Girls and Twilight Lovers*. New York: Penguin, 1991.

Fetterley, Judith. *The Resisting Reader: A Feminist Approach to American Fiction*. Bloomington: Indiana University Press, 1978.

Field, Andrew. *Djuna: The Life and Times of Djuna Barnes*. New York: Putnam, 1983.

Fifer, Elizabeth. *Rescued Readings: A Reconstruction of Gertrude Stein's Difficult Texts*. Detroit: Wayne State University Press, 1992.

Foucault, Michel. *The History of Sexuality, Volume 1: An Introduction*. New York: Vintage Books, 1990.

Freedman, Estelle B., Barbara C. Gelpi, Susan L. Johnson and Kathleen M. Weston, eds. *The Lesbian Issue: Essays from Signs*. Chicago: University of Chicago Press, 1984.

Friedman, Susan. *Psyche Reborn: The Emergence of H.D*. Bloomington: Indiana University Press, 1981.

———.and Rachel Blau DuPlessis. "'I had two loves separate': The Sexualities of H.D.'s *Her*." *Montemora* 8 (1981): 7-30.

Fuss, Diana, ed. *Inside/Out: Lesbian Theories, Gay Theories*. New York: Routledge, 1991.

Gallop, Jane. *The Daughter's Seduction: Feminism and Psychoanalysis*. Ithaca, N. Y.: Cornell University Press, 1982.

Gilbert, Sandra M., and Susan Gubar. *The Madwoman in the Attic: The Woman Writer and the Nineteenth-Century Literary Imagination*. New Haven, Conn.: Yale University Press, 1984.

———.*No Man's Land: The Place of the Woman Writer in the Twentieth Century, Volume 1: The War of the Words*. New Haven, Conn.: Yale University Press, 1988. *Volume 2: Sexchanges*. New Haven, Conn.: Yale University Press, 1989.

Gould, Jean. *Amy: The World of Amy Lowell and the Imagist Movement*. New York: Dodd, Mead, 1975.

Grahn, Judy. *The Work of a Common Woman: The Collected Poetry of Judy Grahn, 1964-1977*. Trumansburg, N. Y.: Crossing Press, 1978.

————.*Another Mother Tongue: Gay Words, Gay Worlds*. Boston: Beacon Press, 1984.

————.*The Highest Apple: Sappho and the Lesbian Poetic Tradition*. San Francisco: Spinsters Ink, 1985.

————.*Really Reading Gertrude Stein*. Freedom, Calif.: Crossing Press, 1989.

Gregory, Eileen. "Rose Cut in Rock: Sappho and H.D.'s *Sea Garden*." *Contemporary Literature* 27, no. 4 (Winter 1986): 524-544.

————."Scarlet Experience: H.D.'s *Hymen*." *Sagetrieb* 62 (1987): 77-100.

Guest, Barbara. *Herself Defined: The Poet H.D. and her World*. New York: Doubleday, 1984.

H.D. *Bid Me To Live (A Madrigal)*. New York: Dial Press, 1960.

————.*Tribute to Freud*. New York: New Directions, 1974.

————.*End to Torment: A Memoir of Ezra Pound*. Eds. Norman Holmes Pearson and Michael King. New York: New Directions, 1979.

————.*Collected Poems: 1912-1944*. Ed. Louis L. Martz. New York: New Directions, 1983.

————.*HERmione*. New York: New Directions, 1981.

————.*Notes on Thought and Vision*. San Francisco: City Lights Books, 1982.

————.*Asphodel*. Durham, N. C.: Duke University Press, 1992.

————.*Paint It Today*. ed. Cassandra Laity. New York: New York University Press,1992.

————.*Robert Duncan. A Great Admiration: H.D./Robert Duncan Correspondence 1950-1961*. Ed. Robert J. Bertholf. Venice, California:Lapis Press, 1992.

Hoagland, Sarah Lucia. *Lesbian Ethics: Toward New Value*. Palo Alto, Calif.: Institute of Lesbian Studies, 1988.

Hoffman, Michael J., ed. *Critical Essays on Gertrude Stein*. Boston: G. K. Hall, 1986.

Howe, Susan. *My Emily Dickinson*. Berkeley, California: North Atlantic Books, 1985.

Irigaray, Luce. *Speculum of the Other Woman*. Ithaca, N. Y.: Cornell University Press, 1985.

————.*This Sex Which Is Not One*. Ithaca, N. Y.: Cornell University Press, 1985.

Jacobus, Mary, ed. *Women Writing and Writing About Women*. New York: Harper and Row, 1979.

Jay, Karla, and Joanne Glasgow, eds. *Lesbian Texts and Contexts: Radical Revisions*. New York: New York University Press, 1990.

Juhasz, Suzanne. *Naked and Fiery Forms: Modern American Poetry by Women*. New York: Harper and Row, 1976.

————,ed. *Feminist Critics Read Emily Dickinson*. Bloomington: Indiana University Press, 1983.

Kannestine, Louis F. *The Art of Djuna Barnes: Duality and Damnation*. New York: New York University Press, 1977.

Katz, Johnathan. *Gay American History: Lesbians and Gay Men in the USA*. New York: Crowell, 1976.

Kouidis, Virginia. *Mina Loy: American Modernist Poet*. Baton Rouge: Louisiana State University Press, 1980.

Kristeva, Julia. *The Kristeva Reader*. Ed. Toril Moi. New York: Columbia University Press, 1987.

Laity, Cassandra. "H.D.'s Romantic Landscapes: The Sexual Politics of the Garden." *Sagetrieb* 6 (1987): 57-75.

Liston, Maureen R. *Gertrude Stein: An Annotated Critical Bibliography*. Kent: Kent State University Press, 1979.

Lorde, Audre. *The Black Unicorn*. New York: W. W. Norton, 1978.

————.*Sister Outsider*. Trumansburg, N. Y.: Crossing Press, 1984.

Lowell, Amy. *The Complete Poetical Works of Amy Lowell*. Boston: Houghton Mifflin, 1955.

Loy, Mina. *The Last Lunar Baedeker*. ed. Roger L. Conover. Highlands: Jargon Society, 1982.

———. *The Lost Lunar Baedeker*. ed. Roger L. Conover. New York, N. Y.: Farrar, Straus and Giroux, 1996.

Marks, Elaine, and Isabelle de Courtivron, eds. *New French Feminisms*. New York: Schocken, 1981.

Meese, Elizabeth A. *Crossing the Double-Cross: The Practice of Feminist Criticism*. Chapel Hill: University of North Carolina Press, 1986.

Miller, Nancy K., ed. *The Poetics of Gender*. New York: Columbia University Press, 1986.

Mitchell, Juliet, and Jacqueline Rose, eds. *Jacques Lacan and the Ecole Freudienne: Feminine Sexuality*. New York: W. W. Norton, 1982.

Moi, Toril. *Sexual/Textual Politics: Feminist Literary Theory*. New York: Methuen, 1985.

Nestle, Joan. *A Restricted Country*. Ithaca, N. Y.: Firebrand, 1987.

O'Neal, Hank. *"Life is painful, nasty, and short—in my case it has only been painful and nasty."* New York: Paragon House, 1990.

Ostriker, Alicia. "What Do Women (Poets) Want: H.D. and Marianne Moore as Poetic Ancestresses." *Poesis* 6, nos. 3-4 (Fall 1985):1-9.

———. *Stealing the Language: The Emergence of Women's Poetry in America*. Boston: Beacon Press, 1986.

Perloff, Marjorie. *The Poetics of Indeterminacy: Rimbaud to Cage*. Princeton, N. J.: Princeton University Press, 1981.

Pharr, Suzanne. *Homophobia, A Weapon of Sexism*. Inverness, Calif.: Chardon, 1988.

Plumb, Cheryl J. *Fancy's Craft: Art and Identity in the Early Works of Djuna Barnes*. Selinsgrove, Penn.: Susquehanna University Press, 1986.

Porter, David T. *The Art of Emily Dickinson's Early Poetry*. Cambridge, Mass.: Harvard University Press, 1966.

Quinn, Vincent. *Hilda Doolittle (H.D.)*. New York: Twayne, 1967.

Raymond, Janice G. *A Passion for Friends: Toward a Philosophy of Female Affection*. Boston: Beacon Press, 1986.

Reagon, Bernice Johnson. "Coalition Politics: Turning The Century." In *Home Girls: A Black Feminist Anthology*, ed. Barbara Smith. New York: Kitchen Table: Women of Color Press, 1983.

Rich, Adrienne. *The Dream of a Common Language: Poems 1974-1977*. New York: W.W. Norton, 1978.

———. *On Lies, Secrets and Silences: Selected Prose, 1966-1978*. New York: W. W. Norton, 1979.

———. *Blood, Bread and Poetry: Selected Prose 1979-1985*. New York: W. W. Norton, 1986.

Rothenberg, Jerome. *Revolution of the Word: A New Gathering of American Avant Garde Poetry 1914-1945*. New York: Seabury Press, 1974.

Ruddick, Lisa. "A Rosy Charm: Gertrude Stein and the Repressed Feminine." In Hoffman, *Critical Essays on Gertrude Stein*. Boston: G. K. Hall, 1986.

———. *Reading Gertrude Stein: Body Text, Gnosis*. Ithaca, N. Y.: Cornell University Press, 1990.

Rule, Jane. *Lesbian Images*. Garden City, N. Y.: Doubleday, 1975.

Scott, James B. *Djuna Barnes*. Boston: Twayne Publishers, 1976.

Secor, Cynthia. "Gertrude Stein: The Complex Force of Her Femininity." In *Women, the Arts, and the 1920's in Paris and New York*, eds. Kenneth W. Wheeler and Virginia Lee Lussier. New Brunswick, N. J.: Rutgers University Press, 1982.

Showalter, Elaine, ed. *The New Feminist Criticism: Essays on Women, Literature and Theory*. New York: Pantheon Books, 1985.

Stein, Gertrude. *The Autobiography of Alice B. Toklas*. New York: Vintage Books, 1960.

————.*Selected Writings of Gertrude Stein*. Ed. Carl Van Vechten. New York: Vintage Books, 1972.

————.*The Yale Gertrude Stein*. Ed. Richard Kostelanetz. New Haven, Conn.: Yale University Press, 1980.

————.*Lifting Belly*. Ed. Rebecca Mark. Tallahassee Fla.: Naiad Press, 1989.

Stimpson, Catherine R. "The Mind, the Body, and Gertrude Stein." *Critical Inquiry 3* (1977): 489-506.

————"Gertrice/Altrude: Stein, Toklas, and the Paradox of the Happy Marriage." In *Mothering the Mind*, eds. Ruth Perry and Martine Watson Brownley. New York: Holmes and Meyer, 1984.

————"The Somagrams of Gertrude Stein." *Poetics Today 6*, nos. 1-2 (1985): 67-80.

————"Gertrude Stein and the Transposition of Gender." In *The Poetics of Gender*, ed. Nancy K. Miller. New York: Columbia University Press, 1986.

Swann, Thomas Burnett. *The Classical World of H.D.* Lincoln: University of Nebraska Press, 1962

Thacker, Andrew. "Amy Lowell and H.D.: The Other Imagists." *Women: A Cultural Review* 4, no. 1 (Spring 1993): 47-59.

Tompkins, Jane, ed. *Reader Response Criticism: From Formalism to Post-Structuralism*. Baltimore: Johns Hopkins University Press, 1980.

Walker, Barbara. *The Women's Encyclopedia of Myths and Secrets*. San Francisco: Harper and Row, 1983.

Watts, Emily S. *The Poetry of American Women from 1632-1945*. Austin: University of Texas Press, 1977.

Wittig, Monique. *The Lesbian Body*. New York: Avon, 1973.

————.*Les Guerilleres*. Boston: Beacon Press, 1985.

————.*The Straight Mind and Other Essays*. Boston: Beacon Press, 1992.

Wolfe, Susan J., and Julia Penelope, eds. *Sexual Practice/Textual Theory: Lesbian Cultural Criticism*. Cambridge, Mass.: Basil Blackwell, 1993.

Woolf, Virginia. *A Room of One's Own*. New York: Harcourt Brace Jovanovich, 1957.

Index

About the Author

MARY E. GALVIN has been teaching literature, writing, and women's studies at the State University of New York, Albany, for the past nine years. Her specialization is in lesbian and gay studies, and poetry, particularly women's poetry.

ISBN 0-313-29810-6

90000>

9 780313 298103

HARDCOVER BAR CODE